The Chinese Economy

Jan Deleyne

The Chinese Economy

Translated from the French by
ROBERT LERICHE

 ANDRE DEUTSCH

First published 1973 by
André Deutsch Limited
105 Great Russell Street, London WC1

Copyright © 1973 English translation
by André Deutsch Limited

Originally published in French under the title
L'Economie Chinoise

© 1971 by Editions du Seuil, Paris
All rights reserved

Printed in Great Britain by
Ebenezer Baylis and Son Limited
The Trinity Press, Worcester, and London

ISBN 0 233 96418 5

Contents

I liked everything about it (China) . . . the intensity of the specifically human quality and especially what I would call umanità.

PAUL CLAUDEL

MAIN CHINESE MEASURES AND EQUIVALENTS

The *li* is 500 metres, or about 540 yards. The *mu* is 666 square metres, or a sixth of an acre. As regards the coinage, the *yuan* = $0·425 (January 1973). One *yuan* = 10 *mao* = 100 *fen*.

Billion in the text is equivalent to one thousand million (not one million million).

Introduction

Now that the cultural revolution of 1967–68 is a thing of the past, it is possible, for the first time for some years, to see the Chinese economy in perspective, and even to hazard a forecast of its future evolution without too much fear of being completely belied by events. For one thing, the sound and fury of that revolution has died down, and a new normality has emerged.[1] There have been no violent changes in the structure of the economy, and the country's economic objectives are the same as those which were forged at the time of China's quarrel with the USSR. If anything, even greater emphasis is laid on them. China, now as then, is determined to secure economic independence and nuclear power.

Curiously enough, too, the cultural revolution has resulted in a fuller flow of information on internal party discussions, including those following the Great Leap Forward of 1958 and 1959. Most of this information is derived from the newspapers of the Red Guards and the posters in which the students and workers in particular vigorously expressed their views on current events. Unlike the leaders of the other socialist countries, Mao Tse-tung[2] did not keep the revolution within the narrow bounds of the party organs but carried it into the street and appealed to the 'masses', who responded enthusiastically.

As against this, the party press concentrated on the destructive rather than on the constructive aspects of the cultural revolution. Thus, little information has been vouchsafed on the reformation of the productive units or on wage policy, the role of the revolutionary committees in the factories or the contents of the annual or Five

1. This statement refers to the economic and not the military situation. According to foreigners who have visited the country after the cultural revolution, China is rather like an armed camp where the citizens are being urged to prepare for a war of aggression by digging air raid shelters in every town and village.
2. We have used the Wade system of transcription which is prevalent in the West.

Year Plans to which frequent reference is made. As a result, the cultural revolution has made it more difficult to grasp the working of the economic mechanisms and in particular to decide how effective they are.

Nor did our knowledge of the levels of production in the different sectors improve between 1966 and 1971. Analysts were thrown back, more than ever, on conjectures, since the Chinese authorities kept their production figures secret, probably because they had only a vague idea of the statistics for agriculture and for small and medium scale industry.

The situation did not change till February 1971, when Chou En-lai granted an interview to the late Edgar Snow, a United States journalist, on behalf of the Italian weekly *Epoca*. Snow was able to penetrate the statistical veil, thanks largely to the confidence the Chinese leaders had in him as the first to have discerned (as far back as 1935) the potential importance of their movement. He thus obtained the earliest official figures on the level of economic activity to have been published since 1960.

These figures cover the total value of industrial and agricultural output as well as the quantities produced of five of the main commodities – cereals, steel, oil, fertilisers and cotton fabrics. It is to be hoped that the Prime Minister's disclosures to Mr Snow presage the resumption of the regular publication of complete statistics, as was the practice prior to 1960. The production figures for the years from 1960 to 1970, however, are likely to remain a mystery.

In most cases, Chou En-lai's figures confirm previous estimates. These were 240 million tons of cereals, 18 million tons of steel, over 20 million tons of oil and 8·5 million metres of cotton fabrics. The only point at which the conjectures seriously differ from the Prime Minister's figures is in relation to fertilisers, where production is stated to be in the neighbourhood of 14 million tons as against the general estimate of 8 to 10 million tons.

But Chou En-lai's figures are well above the estimates for the value of agricultural and industrial production, which he put at 90 and 30 billion US dollars respectively. (The figure for industry includes transport.) They are 50% higher than the estimate by the Japanese Foreign Ministry for 1969, which suggested a maximum of 80 billion dollars. To obtain an estimate of the gross national product, we must add the figures for trade and services, and include such items as the construction of private dwellings and work on irrigation. If, however, we exclude these items, the *per capita* income, according to Chou En-lai, is about 160 dollars.

The progress reflected in these figures is considerable. We need merely recall that the official Chinese statistics put the gross national product at 28 billion dollars in 1952 and 44 billion in 1958. The growth is therefore 170%, but that is measured in current prices, and would naturally be less in terms of constant prices. Whatever the yardstick, the growth was particularly impressive in the case of industry.

What other sources are there from which to supplement these official data on China? There are of course the photographs taken by the US observation satellites, which would no doubt be highly instructive if they were made available. The unprivileged analyst can derive much more profit from a source which almost dried up during the cultural revolution, and which has again started to prove productive. This source is provided by the foreigners who, since 1970, in gradually increasing numbers, have been allowed to enter China, have visited factories, communes, universities, research institutes, and have been able to talk with politicians, economists and civil servants. As might be expected, the Japanese were to the fore in this connection, since Japan is China's main commercial partner.

The occasions for visits by the Japanese have been various – the negotiation of contracts with the State commercial corporations at the Canton Fair, and participation in exhibitions of their country's industrial products at Peking or Shanghai.

These Japanese sources provide the most abundant and the most detailed information on the Chinese economic situation. During the cultural revolution, too, it was the Japanese journalists in Peking who, thanks to their knowledge of the language, reaped the richest harvest of documents, especially the Red Guards' papers and the wall posters, many of which had to be quickly deciphered before they were plastered over by other posters.

I do not feel, however, that visitors to China after the cultural revolution managed to obtain such a wealth of data as their predecessors. After Jan Myrdal's trip to China in 1962, he filled page after page with figures. But a stay of several weeks in the same commune in Shen-si in 1969 was quite unfruitful because of alleged 'reasons of security' and also because, he was told, 'nobody now takes the trouble to record figures'. 'We no longer keep this kind of statistics,' he was informed by the Chairman of the Revolutionary

Committee who, before the cultural revolution, was the head of the brigade. 'The discussion is not yet over, and the masses have not yet taken a decision,' Myrdal was told when he pressed the point.

The decade from 1960 to 1970 can be defined as 'the silent decade'. At an earlier stage, the regime was not so secretive. Thus, Peking published a document called *Ten Great Years* (1950–1960). Thanks to this collection of economic statistics, which was the only Chinese source available, we possess data for the pre-1960 national income, its distribution between the primary, secondary and tertiary sectors, investments by type, employment and its distribution, and population, in addition to the main categories of production. The value and accuracy of these data have been contested. It has been argued that China's data-collecting system was too poor to provide reliable figures. Nevertheless, the statistics in *Ten Great Years* show the main lines along which the economy developed, at least up to 1957. From 1958 on, this information was notoriously distorted by the over-zealousness of the statisticians at all levels. Their mistakes have been admitted and corrected by the Chinese authorities themselves, but even the amended official statistics for 1958 and 1959 are still inflated.

Since then, no official publication has been issued. We are therefore reduced, for the Sixties, to relying on extrapolations, conjectures, estimates and cross-checks with substantial margins of approximation.

Thus, we are not so well informed about the size of the population as the Dutch East India Ambassadors who, on their arrival in China in 1665, were shown the results of a recent census.[1] In 1970, China's population can be estimated only to the nearest 100 million. When it comes to the main products, estimates for 1967 vary according to the source from 185 to 230 million tons for cereals, from 170 to 250 million tons for coal, from 8·5 to 15 for oil and from 9 to 15 for steel.

When the Third Five Year Plan was announced in 1965, the Chinese authorities did not reveal the figures for their targets. Perhaps they were afraid that they might damage the regime's prestige by publishing results occasionally less favourable than those for 1958 and 1959, even when rectified downwards. The Government was badly bitten during the Great Leap Forward, when the local

1. 'If you are prepared to credit the Histories of China . . . you will find that the population is about 58,914,284 men (excluding the Royal Family, the Magistrates, the Eunuchs, the Sacrificers and the Women and Children).'

12

party cadres deliberately confused achievements with targets. It was therefore presumably shy of repeating the same mistake and of resuming the publication of statistics before the necessary data-collecting machinery had been set up.

In default of hard facts, we were until recently obliged to turn to other Chinese sources such as editorials and official handouts, whether broadcast or published in the national or provincial press. But this material needs careful interpretation.

It is dangerous, too, to try to construct aggregates, or a model of the whole Chinese economy, as a number of exercises may provide seemingly precise figures, but that does not make them any more reliable. It is surely pointless, for example, to try and estimate the distribution of investment as between the various sectors of production for the years after the Great Leap Forward. And who could have claimed, before Chou En-lai's disclosures to Edgar Snow, even on the basis of detailed computations, to be able to calculate the Gross National Product (which may range from 80 to 120 billion dollars) or the *per capita* output of a country whose population we can only approximately estimate?

The truth about China is not to be found only in dubious statistics, but also in the observations of visitors able to grasp the economic and social reality of the country. Sources of this kind are fairly plentiful. In addition to the works of Professors René Dumont and Charles Bettelheim, for example, we can draw on the accounts of numerous journalists, scholars, engineers and businessmen who have spent some time in China and have asked questions which have been answered, more often than is generally believed, with good will and precision. However, such information has usually to pass through Chinese interpreters who, though generally excellent, find their skill severely taxed by the translation of technical expressions and figures, especially as the Chinese count by 10,000. Another frequent cause of confusion is that the rice yield is often given without any indication of whether the figure refers to paddy or husked rice. Howlers both in syntax and vocabulary are not infrequent. Thus, visitors were informed that since the liberation the fish were red, when what was meant was merely that the new regime had filled the basins of Hang-Chow with goldfish (*poissons rouges*). It sometimes happens, too, that, in order to evade a question, the Chinese involved gives an irrelevant reply or, so as not to admit his ignorance, simply makes up an answer.

While bearing in mind these sources of error, we shall utilise accounts of visits to factories and people's communes. On such occasions, the Chinese management, during the preliminary conversation round the traditional teapot or during the visit itself, gave valuable indications about the way their organisation was run. They might, for example, inform the visitor of the financial balance sheet of the undertaking, together with the turnover, the total wage bill, the social welfare fund, the investment fund and the taxes and profits transferred to the State.

Even so, we should be careful not to generalise on the basis of the specific experience of foreign visitors. In the case of the system of labour remuneration, for example, the difference between the various situations in the 74,000 people's communes and the autonomy granted to the production teams are such that it is difficult to say which is the most commonly used formula.

Nevertheless, information obtained on the spot is often valuable. We know for example that, since 1965, Chinese engineers have been able to produce oxygen steel, to bring the temperature of the air up to 1250° in blast furnaces, and to manufacture electronic microscopes, 12,000-ton hydraulic presses, and Diesel locomotives.

Nevertheless we must endeavour, however cautiously, to answer the general questions asked about any economy. What is the present population, and how will it grow in the coming decades? What prospects of employment can the State offer to the generations who, in increasing numbers, are coming on the labour market? When will China's agriculture be able to feed and clothe the people? When will the economy grow fast enough to raise the standard of living and the rate of investment? When will science and technology draw level with those of countries such as Britain and France?

The answers to these questions will help to set in perspective the options open to China's foreign policy. Will the country continue to fall back on itself, as so often in its history, and develop on autarkic lines, while claiming to be the only revolutionary centre in a world in which Russia has 'defected'? Or will it take its place in the concert of nations, as the USSR strove to do some years after the October Revolution?

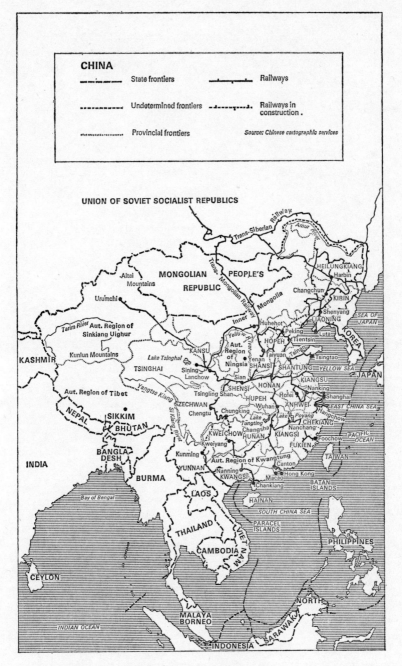

China and South East Asia

1. The Chinese economy before the Cultural Revolution

On a blank page everything is possible.
One can write on it whatever is newest
and finest.

Mao Tse-tung

For an understanding of China's economic policy before the cultural revolution, a brief outline of the country's economic and human factors is essential.

The handicaps

From the economic point of view, China is not in a particularly favourable situation compared, for example, with the USSR. Like India, it is one of the poorest countries in the world, despite its ancient civilisation and its contribution to technological progress before the advent of the modern world. Admittedly, it has recently made considerable progress and, according to Chou En-lai, it has raised its *per capita* income to about $170 (in 1970), but it is still near the bottom of the world league in terms of wealth. The population has always been too dense for the amount of cultivated land, and is concentrated in a few regions of mild climate and fertile soil. Huge areas are left fallow. The fertile regions have always given the impression of being skilfully and thoroughly farmed: 'They do not allow an inch of land to stay fallow or untilled,' wrote the Ambassadors of the Dutch East India Company in 1665. The same observers faithfully reflect the impressions of contemporary visitors to China when they note that it is 'a country so heavily populated' that the traveller seems to see 'fairs and encamped armies' on every side, or when they recall that the Portuguese, on first entering the kingdom, wondered 'whether the women did not produce nine or ten children at a time'.

The density of population on a restricted cultivable area, and the resultant low level of income, sharply distinguish China from the USSR, whose *per capita* income in 1928 (when its first Five Year Plan was launched) was three or even four times as high as China's in 1952. It is clear why the USSR found it easier to skim off from agriculture the funds needed to develop its industry. How substantial these agricultural surpluses were may be judged from the fact that, from 1913 to 1932, the grain harvest fell (as a result of the Great War and internal disturbances) from 82 to 63 million tons, yet the amount marketed remained more or less stable and fell only slightly, from 21 to 20 million tons.

It may be argued that overpopulation did not prevent Japan from modernising from 1867 on. But it is not generally realised that, during the first forty years of the Meiji epoch, the average population growth was under 1% a year and that it was only after 1910 that the State encouraged people to have more children as part of an imperialistic policy. The Japanese were always careful to keep population within the limits imposed by the cultivable area available, and therefore long practised birth control mainly in the form of infanticide. In China, where infanticide was restricted to girls, population growth began to endanger economic equilibrium as early as the eighteenth century, and underlay the social disturbances in the nineteenth.

China's sheer vastness constitutes another disadvantage. The growth of production is restricted by the transport bottleneck. This situation has always been noticeable, and continued to be a negative factor, for example, in the Great Leap Forward and in the extensive internal migrations caused by the cultural revolution. In contrast, Japan was greatly assisted by the smallness of its territory and by the fact that it is a group of islands, which greatly facilitates internal communications.

When it comes to mineral resources, it is common knowledge that China is poorly endowed in comparison with the United States or the USSR. However, the reserves of the main raw materials appear to be sufficient for present needs, except for nickel, platinum, copper and chrome. New discoveries will probably be made as prospecting is stepped up. In fact, the search for fresh resources, which is being energetically pursued, has already produced impressive results. The Government has in a short space of time trained numerous geologists whom it has despatched over its whole territory, with special emphasis on the desert and outlying regions. For the moment it is hazardous to make any forecast about China's resources, as the case of oil illustrates. Reserves of that commodity were assumed to be very low in 1949, but today they are believed to be considerable.

Assets

As against this modest endowment in natural resources, China has a number of assets which most underdeveloped countries lack, and which are much more difficult to acquire than is sometimes believed by those who seek to copy the Chinese model.

The brilliance of its civilisation and the talents of its people have earned admiration in every age. Even so, it is not generally known that up to the end of the European Middle Ages China was the main world source of scientific and technical invention, and that Europe has borrowed much more from it than China from Europe.

China was the first country in the world to be governed by civil servants who represented the State even in the most distant provinces, and who saw to the execution of the central authorities' orders. When the Communists assumed power, this bureaucratic tradition was invaluable in a State where order had to be restored. The Communist Party was in fact able to act with the assent of a population accustomed to accepting orders from above.

The stages of collectivisation

When a regime professing Marxist-Leninist tenets came to power, the socialisation of the means of production was bound to follow sooner or later. In China, the process took place in several stages. The State and the party assumed control of the economy. In industry, mixed and private sectors were allowed to exist side by side for some time. In agriculture, the transition was effected in the course of a few years from cooperatives, where each member remained the owner of his land, to the socialist cooperative where the land was common property, with the exception of the relatively tiny family plots.

One of the first aims of the new leaders was to make China an industrial power. They have not succeeded in doing so in the short period which they set themselves, but this is still their long-term objective, even if in 1961, because of the famine at that time and the rapid increase in population, priority was provisionally given to agriculture.

The regime inherited an agriculture accustomed to traditions and techniques which were not to be transformed overnight. It was to have greater freedom of action in its efforts to apply socialism to the industrial sector. Nevertheless, it proceeded with the greatest

19

caution. Factory owners who stayed on in China after 1949, 'the national capitalists', received from the State a dividend equal to 5% of the nominal value of the capital of the concern which they had owned and in which they often retained administrative functions. These dividends were sometimes considerable. They were mostly invested in State interest-bearing bonds and gave those in possession of them a standard of living well above that of their fellow countrymen. The cultural revolution attacked these privileged individuals. Red Guards' organisations denounced the capitalists who 'battened on the people's blood' and the 'exploiters' whose way of life was a scandal in a socialist China. Although the press and the newspapers did not mention the fact, it is possible that these concessions, which were tacitly extended every five years, were suppressed during the cultural revolution. The Chinese authorities made a point of arranging meetings between foreign visitors and certain of the national capitalists, who were ecstatic about their favoured status which freed them from worrying about economic crises, foreign competition and new outlets for their products. The extent of their privileges can be gauged if they are compared with the *Nepmen* in the USSR who were not guaranteed against bankruptcy, whereas their Chinese opposite numbers were assured a guaranteed income.

Chinese industry was on a very modest scale before 1949. It was far behind Russian industry in 1914, for example. All the same, it was of great importance to the new regime. The proof is that the country's two main industrial centres are still the same as they were when the Revolution took over – namely, the Northeast Region (formerly Manchuria) and Shanghai. China's industry was created largely by foreigners to suit their interests and their requirements. The result has been a lack of balance. Shanghai is at a great distance from the sources of power. Manchurian industry was created from scratch by the Japanese, from 1939 onwards, in a purely agricultural and sparsely populated region. Even today it supplies a third of China's industrial production. The new regime has tried to adjust this unbalance by setting up industries in the less favoured and more neglected regions, although it would have been easier to set them up in the already developed areas. But, up to 1957, when the new factories built with the help of the socialist countries came into production, Chinese industry was conditioned by its pre-1949 heritage, and its output was drawn mainly from old factories which had been restored, modernised and expanded.

From 1949 to 1952, reconstruction was rapid, and the rate of industrial expansion reached the figure of 27% a year.

This achievement is doubtless due to the fact that war damage was not serious and, unlike Japan, China produces most of the raw materials needed for its industry.

The First Five Year Plan (1953–57)

The First Five Year Plan was not published till 1955. It had been prepared with the help of Soviet experts, who submitted to the Chinese a model inspired by their own plan, without fully realising the differences in the conditions of the two countries. Priority was given to industry, and in particular to the heavy and capital goods industry.

At the same time as they were preparing the First Five Year Plan, the Soviet experts were drafting a long-term programme covering three five-year plans which was to provide China in fifteen years' time with an industry which would be coherent and balanced and would meet all the needs of a modern power. Once the 300 factories envisaged by this programme (valued at 3 billion dollars) were built, China would become (by 1967) an independent economic power. In this way, the Russians would have given China an industrial base on which it could build at leisure, using its own resources.

This long-term programme got off to a promising start. The annual rate of growth was 14%, and industrial output doubled, or almost, in five years. If we exclude 1953, which can be regarded as the last year of reconstruction, when the rate was 25%, the increase was 12% a year from 1954 to 1957.

With the return of peace and with the help of the socialist countries, China showed what it was capable of, and was, it seemed, about to follow the course taken by the USSR thirty years earlier. It had fallen far behind, but it looked as if the Chinese people, spurred on by a totalitarian and egalitarian regime, would be able to catch up in the foreseeable future.

The Great Leap Forward (1958–60)

Why did China not continue along this path but decide on the experiment of the Great Leap Forward? The 'model pupils' – to use

21

Mao's own expression – turned into unruly youngsters who regarded their Soviet teachers as timorous greybeards, wedded to
excessively cautious rates of development and lacking confidence in
the Chinese people.

The rates of expansion aimed at by the Great Leap Forward were
totally unrealistic. Many of the figures published were absurd, but
found credence among certain western observers. At least some of
the energy generated among the people was certainly wasted. We
know, for example, that the 5–6 million tons of steel produced in the
rural blast furnaces proved unusable. All the same, great progress
was made in the years 1958–60. The factories started during the
First Plan came into production. Of the 921 major projects undertaken under that Plan, 428 were completed by the end of 1957 and
had gone into production. Of the rest, 109 were on the way to
completion and in partial production. In 1958, 500 new projects
were completed and many others initiated. The Great Leap Forward
saw the preparation of the blueprints for a number of factories. It
was therefore not surprising that Chinese industry should have
made great progress from 1958 on. The exact extent of the advance
is not known. Estimates of the annual rate of expansion put it at
31% in 1958, 26% in 1959 and 4% in 1960, giving an average of
20% a year for the Great Leap Forward, compared with one of 14%
for the First Five Year Plan.

The Great Leap Forward fell short of its objectives for a great
many reasons. There were the poor harvests, due to natural
calamities, which created a scarcity of food in the towns; a drop in
productivity in the factories and a dearth of agricultural raw
materials which affected output in light industry. A number of
machines were worked to death, broke down and became un-
serviceable. In any case, the frantic rhythm imposed on industry
could not possibly be kept up for long. The transport bottleneck also
acted as a brake on industry. The railways were unable to cope with
the increased traffic in raw materials.

Lastly, the departure of the Soviet experts was a decisive factor in
the collapse of industry. Since 1957, the two countries were at
loggerheads over foreign policy and atomic weapons. All the same,
the Chinese did not expect a fraternal socialist country to abandon
them quite so suddenly. They could not believe that State rivalries
would prevail over ideological solidarity and proletarian internationalism.

22

'Readjustment' (1961–66)

In 1961, the Communist party central committee recommended that henceforth the four principles of 'readjustment, consolidation, reinforcement and improvement' should be applied. They thus admitted the need for a pause in order to repair the country's strength and to permit the recovery of men exhausted by intensive physical labour, of land over-farmed, and of equipment worked well beyond its normal capacity.

From then on, agriculture was the 'basis of the economy', which meant that the economy could not expand unless agriculture was thriving enough to feed the population and to provide light industry with raw materials. This appears quite logical in a nation in which over 80% of the population lives in the countryside, and famine has always raised its head as soon as population pressure became excessive. However, industry remained the decisive factor in the new economic policy inaugurated in 1960. In other words, while it was essential to have a thriving agriculture, this was not sufficient to ensure that China would become a powerful modern nation. Agriculture feeds men and women, but industry alone supplies the tools for achieving productivity, including that of agriculture, and also the weapons which constitute the strength of States. Light industry, for its part, was rated higher than heavy industry since it had to satisfy some at least of the consumer needs of the population, which had been sorely tried by the hard years after the Great Leap Forward.

Industry was therefore not neglected after the 1959–61 famine obliged the Government to pay more attention to agriculture. It made considerable progress which, however, varied as between different branches. Heavy industry, which usually enjoys a privileged position in socialist regimes, was given a share of investment which was much the same as in the First Five Year Plan. It is probable that, on the eve of the cultural revolution, coal and steel production had not caught up with the figure for 1960. In 1965, the output of coal, which supplies the bulk of the energy consumed in China, had still not risen to 250 or 300 million tons at most. It was officially 424 million tons in 1960, but this figure was 100 million tons above the real one, and included many unusable and poor quality types of coal from small, hastily improvised mines. The same applies to steel. The 18·6 million tons of which China boasted in 1960 included, according to official sources, 5 to 6 million tons produced by the country blast furnaces which were mostly unusable. The real figure was probably 13 million tons. It is possible that, in 1966, output came close to this figure. Estimates vary from 12 to 14 million tons or above. On the other hand, two sectors have registered considerable progress since 1960 – oil and fertilisers.

As regards industrial output, the figure for 1965 appears to be slightly higher than that for 1958, the first year of the Great Leap Forward, but definitely below the 1960 figure which marked the zenith of Chinese economic development (88% over 1956). In short, it is argued that industry, after having been borne upwards by three years of the Great Leap Forward to a level 80% above that for 1957, and after having fallen back in 1962 to a level equal to that in 1957, had not yet succeeded in 1965 in catching up even approximately with the higher level attained in 1960. Hence the conclusion of certain economists, as peremptory as it is over-simple, that 'the Great Leap Forward cost China ten years' growth, and Chinese industry has been thrown back to the point reached before that movement began'. This is to forget that, even if the volume of production was no higher in 1965 than in 1959, the economy was much less vulnerable because much nearer to the goal of independence.

Up to 1960, the Chinese leaders, realising how far their country lagged behind, and conscious of their need for foreign aid, were content to be a brilliant second to the USSR in the socialist camp. In a speech in 1956, Chou En-lai admitted that China would still have to rely, for many years to come, on help from the USSR and the peoples' democracies. 'It is difficult', he said, 'to imagine that we can coop ourselves up and do without aid.' Neither in the socialist camp nor in capitalist countries did anyone ever imagine in 1958–59 that China could, overnight, develop its economy single-handed. The Chinese were the first to grasp the fact that Soviet aid was the basis on which their development rested, and that it determined their rate of progress. In consequence, the first disagreements over policy did not affect economic cooperation.

Today the position has changed radically. The Chinese, who in 1960 depended on the Soviet technicians to run their factories properly, have succeeded in a few years in mastering the production process, and have attained technical and financial independence. All the factories at present functioning in China are the result of

Chinese engineering skill alone. The Chinese have elevated this industrial takeover to the dignity of a dogma, though it was forced on them by the departure of the Soviet experts, and have termed it in their own language 'counting only on their own strength', or, in other words, self-reliance.

Making a virtue of necessity, the Chinese leaders appealed to national feeling and denounced the Soviet 'treason'. They urged their people to take in hand the productive apparatus from which the foreign experts had just withdrawn and show the world that China had no need of help to manage and develop its economy. Jealous of the country's international reputation, the country's leaders, far from repudiating their debts to a country which in their eyes had gone back on its word by suddenly ending contractual aid, made it a point of honour to repay their debts to the USSR ahead of time – and they did so in full by the end of 1964.

These Chinese engineers and workers, asked by their leaders to manage themselves the often complex machines and equipment which had been set up by the Russians, responded to the appeal. Spurred on by the Soviet defection and by pride, they succeeded, after some initial fumblings and setbacks, in mastering the techniques and acquiring the necessary know-how. The years following the Russians' departure were used in getting the machines and factories going. To start with, these humble efforts had only a slight impact on production.

But the objective in view was not a quantitative one. The important point was to set the wheels turning. It was an uphill battle, but by 1964 industrial output once again registered substantial progress.

No sizeable financial investment was involved, or the creation of large new factories. According to statements by the Prime Minister in December 1964, the rate of industrial growth in 1964 over 1963 was 15%, and it was expected to be 11% in 1965. For 1966, an increase of 20% over 1965 was announced in September and confirmed in December 1966 at the traditional stock-taking at the end of the year. This high growth rate in 1966, the first year of the cultural revolution, is perhaps to be explained by the desire to prove that that movement had inspired the Chinese people with an increased ardour to work hard.

The Third Plan (1966–70)

Nothing has been published about the main objectives of the Third Plan (1966–70) or, *a fortiori*, about the production targets. The secret has been well kept, and the indications obtained from different sources do not tally. Information from Chinese refugees in Hong Kong suggests that the annual growth rates in the Plan were 2 to 3% for agriculture and 5 to 7% for industry. These figures seem modest when set against the ambitious aims of the Chinese leaders and their haste to make their country a first-rate economic power. Figures obtained in China itself appear more probable. The annual rates of growth, according to this source, are 4·4% for agriculture and 12% for industry (9 for coal, 11 for steel, 12 for oil and 15 for fertilisers and electricity).[1]

The rate of 12% for industry is lower than that of 14% in the First Plan, which is normal if we accept the fact that the rates for the initial periods, where the starting point is very low, cannot be kept up. It should not be forgotten that the growth in the First Plan owed a great deal to the Soviet aid of which China is now deprived. Moreover, the unused capacity, the return of which to production has made possible the progress of over 10% registered in 1964 and 1965, has fallen off sharply, and the maintenance of a growth rate of over 10% would presuppose the creation of new factories and hence of new investment. Is the present rate of investment sufficient for that purpose? It seems to be about 20% of the gross national product, but certain writers put the share of military equipment at 10 or even 12%, i.e. half or more of that proportion. If that is the case, the rate of investment is insufficient to ensure an annual increase of over 10%. However, in default of massive introduction of modern equipment, the economy can benefit from technological investments flowing, for example, from the application of improved manufacturing processes or from savings in raw materials. There is considerable scope for the improvement of productivity along these lines, especially in small and medium enterprises which are being set up or expanded throughout the country in accordance with the government's directives.

1. According to the Prime Minister's declaration to Edgar Snow in February 1971, the targets of the Third Plan were, by and large, met, and indeed several of them were amply exceeded. The size of industrial output in 1970 – 90 billion dollars according to Chou En-lai – bears witness to the dominant position now attained by industry.

The Fourth Plan (1971–75)

On the basis of information provided by the Chinese press and radio since the start of the Fourth Five Year Plan, it is possible to make out the Plan's priority objectives. In the industrial field, the main effort is in heavy industry – iron and steel (especially the extraction of iron ore), hydrocarbons and chemical fertilisers. Agriculture still remains the basis of the economy, to use the standard expression. But no information has been issued officially on the Plan's contents.

2. The management and organisation of the economy up to the Cultural Revolution

The fundamental aim of our great revolution
is to liberate the productive forces of
our country from the oppression of imperialism,
feudalism, bureaucratic capitalism, and, lastly,
from the bonds of capitalism and small
scale production, so as to allow our national
economy to progress, through planning, rapidly
along the road to socialism.
                    Chou En-lai, 23 September 1954

How is the economy in general, and industry in particular, run at the national and enterprise level? After describing the planning and price policy systems, we will discuss the management of industrial enterprises and the organisation of trade, as well as the living conditions of the workers in modern industry.

Planning – mechanisms and realities

An unusual feature in a socialist regime is that, since 1960, planning covering a number of years is no longer the mainspring of economic development in China. The Great Leap Forward, and subsequently the cultural revolution, put it into cold storage. If, during the period of readjustment from 1961 to 1966, people in the communes and factories still referred to the 'national economic plan', they were thinking of the annual plan. According to a Red Guard newspaper, dated 7 April 1968, the Prime Minister, Chou En-lai, instructed a group of fifty persons (the National Economic Commission) to work out the plan for 1968. At the beginning of 1970, the *Red Flag* mentions the approval, by the central party committee, of the national economic plan for the year. However, reference continued to be made, both in official statements and in the production units, to the Five Year Plan. But the absence of any indication as to the content of the plan suggests that it is merely an agreed framework and is devoid of any of the essential elements of planning.

The planning of the economy was instituted some years after the start of the regime, once the period of reconstruction was over. Its particular merit was that it called for an inventory of resources in a country which had until then been unfamiliar with overall statistics. A Central Statistical Bureau with a staff of 200,000 was founded in 1952, but the data collected by it were still approximative. The statistics were particularly chaotic during the Great Leap Forward, when the local cadres prepared them to measure so that they would tally with the ambitious targets set by the party leaders. This unfortunate experiment led to the abandonment of five-year planning. From then on, the economy was directed only by annual plans, and investment targets were replaced by programmes comprising some seven or eight hundred industrial projects, which it was proposed to implement as opportunity offered, but without any date being fixed for their initiation or for their completion.

One of the reasons why planning was dropped for a period of several years was, as Chinese economists admit, the impossibility of assembling the indispensable statistical data. However, as the economy gradually recovered during the readjustment period, the collection of data was resumed. It was doubtless judged sufficiently satisfactory for a new Five Year Plan (the Third) to be announced for the period 1966–70. The propaganda campaign which usually heralds the launching of a Plan was organised by the party during 1965, thus suggesting the publication of a new Plan at the end of the year. Now, although the start of such a Plan was confirmed at the beginning of 1966, no indication was given of its objectives. For the first time in a socialist regime, a whole people was ordered to embark on a Five Year Plan without being informed of the targets. The dissensions within the party were no doubt the reason for this unwillingness to commit itself.

Once the cultural revolution had died down, the Chinese press and radio again started to mention the annual State Plan, but we are completely in the dark as to its content and the methods used to prepare it. On 1 October 1970, in a traditional speech celebrating the national holiday, the Prime Minister referred to the Fourth Plan (1971–75) but gave no details.

Thus, the principles of planning and their application cover the period *before* the cultural revolution. Our information is taken partly from writers such as Audrey Donnithorne and Yuan Li Wu who have gone into this subject thoroughly.

The Plan is prepared by a dual hierarchy operating at all levels of the administration and the party under the parallel system

29

characteristic of single party socialist regimes. At the higher level, the main role falls to the central party committee and to the Council of State Affairs – an expression which denotes the State Government. That Council controls several commissions including the State Planning Commission, which is responsible for the Five Year Plans, and the State Economic Commission, which looks after the annual plans. At the level of the multi-provincial blocks, which are six in number, and of the districts (*hsien*), of which there are just over 2,000, there are in the same way administrative planning bodies and party planning bodies.

The Plan, it appears, is worked out from the bottom upward, starting from the production unit, be it a factory or a people's commune, and passed on up to the Central Government. Originally, the first stage in the process consisted of the transmission, by the central planning bodies, of a draft plan to the units at the base. The plan was then elaborated where common sense seemed to demand, that is to say, in the production unit itself. A draft quantitative plan for the enterprise or the people's commune is prepared in these units at the instigation, and under the authority, of the party machine which plays a decisive role in the choice and assessment of the targets proposed for the coming year.

This draft plan is the subject of exchanges of views and discussions with the supervising authorities which, depending on the case, can be the district, or, for the large agglomerations of Peking, Shanghai and Tientsin, the town councils. The basic units are thus called upon to make their voice heard in a dialogue, which is a sign (in theory at least) of industrial democracy. But foreign observers have no means of knowing whether this dialogue is in fact uninhibited and whether the basic units really have a chance of carrying their point where they disagree with the supervising authority. The only way of ascertaining the truth on this score would be by collecting evidence from the cadres and the workers of the enterprise themselves, which foreigners are obviously not permitted to do. The non-Chinese observer is thus precluded from examining a field of the greatest interest for an understanding of how the economy works. However there is *some* discussion, and it may be assumed that the Chinese seize this opportunity to have their say, given the patience and talent which they always display in arguments. It appears that one of the aims of the cultural revolution has been to introduce some degree of flexibility into the authoritarian supervision of the production units by the planning bodies, and especially those of the party. If this supposition is correct, the result of the movement has been to give greater scope for discussion to the base, or, as the official jargon puts it, 'to the broad popular masses'. The Chinese Communists' policy, the behaviour of the authorities, and the inborn feeling of the people for compromise, strongly suggest that the base is in fact given a better hearing and a fairer deal than in other socialist regimes.

The basic units' plans are used as the raw material for a double series of plans, some horizontal and multi-sectoral, the others vertical and sectoral. The horizontal plans are finalised by the provincial authorities which include commissions corresponding to the State Planning Commission and the State Economic Commission at the national level, as well as the local offices of the central ministries in Peking. The vertical plans are worked out by the ministries of the Central Government for the sector of production for which they are responsible.

The annual national plan is prepared by the State Economic Commission which coordinates the horizontal and vertical plans and decides on transfers between provinces and sectors. The Plan includes production and marketing targets, by value and volume, for essential commodities, and incorporates plans for foreign trade, investment, manpower and wages, transport, finance and enterprises directly attached to the Central Government.

The provincial planning bodies are responsible for the objectives which are not in the national plan, those, for example, for investments within the competence of the province – local transport, the production of consumer goods, retail trade, housing construction, and so on.

Once the Plan has been finalised by the central planning bodies and approved by the central party committee and then by the Council for State Affairs, the State Plan is transmitted to the authorities at the decentralised administrative levels who are to implement it. According to certain writers, the Plan contains not one estimate but two. One figure represents the minimum which must at all costs be reached, while the other is merely a desirable maximum. The provincial and district authorities, in their turn, transmit the dual targets to be fulfilled to the lower levels. The desirable target received from the Central Government by the province is selected as an imperative target and transmitted to the district level, and so on from the district down to the basic units. But, as we shall see later on, the existence of these alleged dual targets appears to be disproved by statements made in 1970 to foreigners visiting factories.

The provincial authorities do not therefore confine themselves to transmitting the Central Government's instructions to the lower levels. They can decide on an upward revision of the targets fixed by the Centre for the province, and proceed on their own initiative to undertake local investments not provided for in the national Plan. However, the central authorities do not leave the supervision of the Plan's execution entirely in the hands of the provincial authorities. As early as 1959, there was a Ministry of Supervision which exercised this type of control. It has since been suppressed, and it is the party bodies which have taken this task in hand while the ministries send their inspectors to check on the enterprises.

It would be hard to say whether the planning mechanisms are at present functioning in accordance with this ideal model, or indeed whether they ever *have* done. The questions put by visitors to the production units are always given the same answers, which tend to be vague and uninstructive. The plan for the factory or the commune, they are ritually told, is drawn up in the light of the State's needs, which must be given priority. However, the Plan is not imposed by the supervising authorities without previous discussion. It is the fruit of consultations between the higher and the lower levels, and takes account of the conditions specific to each unit. This means that planning observes the principles of democratic centralism. But how is one to know in what way the compromise is reached between the base and the summit, and who makes the greatest concessions?

Admittedly, the Plan is less of a straitjacket than in most socialist countries. Thus, according to the statement of the director of one people's commune, the Plan targets are fixed below the level normally attained, which ensures that they will be exceeded. This latitude left to producers may be regarded as a shrewd move on the part of the central authorities, since it shows that the State has confidence in them and gives them the virtual certainty of being able to do better than they are asked to do.

Even in the more highly industrialised and evolved socialist countries, the planning authorities have not yet succeeded in keeping strict control over the economy as a whole. And this failure is all the more understandable in the case of China, where the modern sector is still relatively undeveloped, small and medium industries are legion, statistics are defective, and government offices are not equipped with computers. The Central Government has to make do with issuing general directives and setting rough targets. In addition, the planning system has not been helped by the serious disturbances which affected the economy in 1959–60 and again in 1966–68. In very many cases, the interruption in the supply of raw materials made nonsense of the planner's forecasts and left him no grounds for complaining about the failure of the efforts to carry out the Plan.

One has the feeling that, with the exception of the large modern factories which come directly under the central ministries in Peking, most plants, especially the small and medium industries, which contribute and will long continue to contribute a large slice of industrial output, have a fairly considerable degree of autonomy. The Central Government puts its trust in them, and counts on achieving the Plan by campaigns launched in quick succession to keep alive revolutionary ardour and industry among the toiling masses.

Ideological stimulants

In the West we are inclined – especially in the United States – to underestimate the beneficent effects on productivity of this permanent stimulation. Judged by western criteria, the regime's obsessional propaganda may appear crude and boring. But, since it is directed at a people which, until recent times, has continued to submit passively to a restrictive social and moral system, it is capable of awakening a feeling for new values. Those who have not had the chance to observe on the spot how seriously the Chinese, whether scientists, engineers or workers, now take the task set them by the regime cannot imagine the enthusiasm with which these people throw themselves into it. This enthusiasm is not, of course, universal, and it is not enough to transform China into a modern nation. Considerable material resources are needed as well. But the self-confidence thus inculcated into the Chinese has been, and still is, an important factor in the transformation of the country.

People have made fun of Mao's thought and the almost miraculous virtues ascribed to it. And there is no doubt that the regime's propaganda often extols it in a way which we find disconcerting. But the catechism of civic virtues contained in the *Little Red Book* is a positive factor. Its effectiveness cannot easily be grasped by westerners who carried out their 'cultural revolution' centuries ago, and who have no idea how backward was the mentality of the peasants and how useful certain elementary verities and childishly simple slogans can be to them. The transformations achieved in a short time by the regime's propaganda can be best brought home by quoting the statement of the director of a people's commune to a foreigner: 'In former times,[1] the peasants attributed plant diseases to the gods and did nothing to combat them. Nowadays, each production team includes a specialist in the identification of the most common diseases and in their treatment. Before the liberation, the peasants believed that it was the Dragon God who controlled the rain, but nowadays they know the scientific explanation.'

Shortage of resources

The regime is more lavish with ideological stimulants than with financial assistance. It seems to be mainly concerned with ensuring that enterprises keep their requests for money for their investments down to the minimum. This is one of the meanings given to the maxim, 'count on your own strength alone', as applied to the production units. Since this slogan was first launched, propaganda has held up as a model the twin examples of Taching for industry and Tachai for agriculture. Both enterprises worked in, or opened up, sterile or desert regions without asking for state assistance, and raised the necessary funds from their own resources. It is this same spirit which impels numerous enterprises to integrate their production. They are afraid of having their stocks run down or of finding that equipment is unavailable, and consequently set about designing and manufacturing the machines themselves, even down to the nuts and bolts. They also make a point of using local raw materials, thus easing the strain on the transport system.

This penury of financial resources is due to the poverty of the country and to the difficulty of increasing the rate of investment. It forces the State to reserve them for priority objectives, and in particular for national defence and the large modern production units. It is probable that, in the case of an enterprise which does not draw on budget funds for its investment, the authorities close an eye to any failure to meet the Plan's targets.

1. That is to say, before the Revolution in 1949.

For the time being, the Chinese economy seems to function largely on autonomous and decentralised lines. Too much so, indeed, for the Government's liking. Moreover, the cultural revolution undermined the authority of the party which, as in all Communist regimes, was the most effective instrument in the execution of the national economic policy and in the supervision of the Plan's implementation. From time to time, therefore, an official statement in the press or on the radio stresses the need to 'establish firm State control' over the production units.

Making the most of present resources

It will, then, be some time before the volume of financial resources is sufficient to foster a rapid rate of growth. Meanwhile, Chinese policy is making the most of the present resources by stimulating the factories to construct the greatest possible variety of equipment, and by vigorously promoting the technical education of the masses. In this way, the country will have at its disposal sufficient skilled manpower against the time when conditions are ripe for a rapid increase in industrial production. Even now, the most modern factories are turning out specialists who can be sent to regions with no industrial background such as Mongolia, Sinkiang and Kansu, or to already developed regions where demand for their services is expanding.

Foreigners are astonished at the low level of specialisation in many of the factories, and at their tendency to manufacture the maximum range of equipment. This policy of producing samples involves a certain dispersal of effort and, to start with, high costs, but the Chinese believe that in the long run it offers the shortest road to economic independence, since thereby workers acquire the maximum know-how in all fields and can, at a pinch, turn their hand to anything. They will come all the closer to this ideal, the more every branch produces at least one prototype for each item in the production chain. It may happen that one of the last items is ready before the previous ones and remains in part unused. But the day will come when the missing links are constructed in their turn and the whole process can function smoothly. A good example of this situation is the development of the 12,000-ton hydraulic press in a factory in the suburbs of Shanghai, built to forge 250-ton ingots. The press produces only 100-ton ingots for lack of a nearby steelworks to supply it with steel. It works only provisionally and at a slow pace. This is unimportant. Its very existence is a success, for it attests the capacity of the Chinese to manufacture a forging press of this size. Its optimal utilisation will come later.

It also happens that a line of manufacture is started on an experimental basis and that it is then given up, once Chinese engineers have proved that they can carry it through successfully. To produce these prototypes, the regime is prepared to pay the necessary price in terms of labour and money, and to completely disregard the cost.

A number of factories have been created out of nothing, sometimes in antiquated repair workshops with machines which had been condemned to the scrap heap. Men without any technical training, often old workmen, have succeeded, often at the cost of lengthy efforts and with great ingenuity, in producing classical-type items. Foreigners who are shown round these primitive factories are disconcerted by the archaic methods, the unsuitability of the machines, which are often manufactured in the factory itself, the confusion in the workshops, the failure to observe even the most elementary rules of safety, the low productivity and the indifference of the management to considerations of cost. And yet, although foreigners are shown only people's communes with a high level of output, access to these factories is as easy as to the most modern industrial establishments. The fact is that, for the Chinese, these workshops illustrate the ability of their workers and technicians to 'count only on their strength' and to 'make something out of nothing.' These achievements, which strike Europeans or Japanese as an economic absurdity, are, for the Chinese, the best guarantee for their industrial future and economic independence. In many respects, they are prouder of them than of the factories inherited from the Russians. In addition, they have the feeling that the 'miracles' produced by the Chinese workers and technicians are up to the expectations of the proletarians of the whole world whose eyes are fixed on China. That, at least, is what a foreign journalist was informed by a model worker, who succeeded in producing high-quality steel in an antiquated converter, thanks to a technique which he affirmed was an entirely new one and confined to China.

The abundance of manpower

Most Chinese factories are overstaffed, and no workers are ever dismissed even when higher productivity would make it possible to use fewer men. The tractor factory at Loyang employs 22,000 persons for an output of what must be from 4,000 to 10,000 45-h.p. tractors a year. The fertiliser factory at Wuching, near Shanghai, employs 2,100 people for an annual production of 100,000 tons of ammoniac sulphate. In short, there are three to four – even ten – times more personnel employed than in European factories for an equivalent production. It is not surprising that in 1966 a Japanese economist estimated Chinese productivity as being six to ten times less than that of his own country.

According to a foreign engineer, the number of supervisors in the dyeing section of a wool-weaving factory he visited was twenty times higher than it would have been in Europe. In a plastic materials factory in Peking, there is one supervisor to every man working the machines. This abundance of manpower sometimes has its advantages. In the electronic hardware factories, for instance, where the controls are far more numerous than in Europe, the percentage of rejects and defective output is very low and the quality of the manufactures excellent.

Handicrafts

It is estimated that a quarter of total industrial output is made up of handicraft products which are traditionally included in Chinese statistics.[1] These products have long succeeded in standing up to competition from modern industrial plants which were set up in China, in the ports open to foreigners, from the end of the nineteenth century. This modern industry did not put an end to handicrafts, which continued to provide the bulk of essential consumer goods. For, contrary to developments in many other countries, handicrafts have survived thanks to the family structure of the enterprise, its ability to produce at extremely low prices, the vastness of the territory and the country's transport difficulties. It is not possible to say how many handicraft workshops there are or how much labour they employ. However, we do know that they produce a wide range of goods, including fabrics and clothes, wickerwork,

---

1. This share was put at 32% in 1949. It declined to 20% in 1952, 14% in 1957 and 10% in 1954. During the Great Leap Forward, numerous artisans were ordered to work in the factories. Since then, the handicrafts sector has been built up again.

toys, plastic wares, small agricultural implements and parts for modern industry for which they often act as subcontractors.

The Chinese economy is still at the stage where its main objective is to produce what is needed by the State, and in particular to meet the vital needs of national defence. It will be readily understood that, in China's present situation, when it is – or imagines it is – encircled by the superpowers acting in collusion and 'preparing to make war on it' as the current slogan has it, considerations of profitability are relegated to the background and may even be considered treasonable.

To attain their objectives, the leaders are counting on the extraordinary degree of self-sacrifice of which the people are capable, and on the vigilance of the army which, since the end of the cultural revolution, seems to be playing a crucial role in running the economy.[1] The problem of measuring efficiency, and in particular profit, will arise at a later stage when China enters an age of plenty. For the moment it would appear that this is still far off. The enterprises have no means of measuring their performance. Compared to productivity in the countries which have long been industrialised, the level is low, and it is not the overriding concern of the authorities to raise it. So long as the equipment and raw materials needed for an increase in production are not available, an increase in productivity would merely reduce the manpower required.

Price policy

Price policy can play a considerable part in a planned socialist economy. The level at which prices are set by the planner determines among other things the profit margins of the production units, as well as the volume and distribution of consumption. Price manipulation can be an effective instrument for planning.

And yet, as far as is known, the Chinese planners do not seem to regard prices as an important policy tool, and they seem cautious about modifying them. For any revision of prices in one sector entails a revision in the others. Moreover, the fixing of prices by rational criteria, in a planned economy, would call for a computer system which the Chinese do not possess.

1. The Communist Chinese army has been obliged, from the moment it was created, to provide all its own supplies. It played an important part in opening up and developing land, especially in the frontier regions.

Hence, prices are fixed empirically, and are generally based on the relations existing before planning was started. This task falls to the administrative bodies – the National Price Commission for the main agricultural and industrial products, and the Provincial or District Commissions for other prices which may vary considerably from one region to another. The only exception to administrative price-fixing is constituted by the free market, which is confined to the rural areas, where the peasants are allowed to sell the produce of their plot. As opposed to the *kolkhoz* markets in the USSR, prices do not appear to be very different from those on the official market.

The administrative commissions apply relatively simple rules to determine prices. Wholesale prices are equal to cost prices, plus a profit margin. Cost prices are calculated on the averages registered in the branch of production in question. The profit margins vary widely depending on the product. They are higher in heavy industry, where they can reach a level of 40 to 100% of the cost price. They are expected to supply the State's budget with the financial resources needed by it, especially for industrial investments. This is their main justification in a system in which the profits of industrial and commercial enterprises accrue to the State.

A characteristic peculiar to China is the emphasis laid on quality. The prices at which goods are purchased from enterprises are determined by the quality of the products as established by the supervisors in the marketing agencies. This policy, combined with the conscientiousness and the dexterity of the workers, explains why, if the replies to visitors' questions are to be believed, rejects are relatively rare, and why the quality of consumption goods is usually higher than in other socialist countries.

Retail prices are fixed by more complex criteria, which take particular account of demand. In principle, these prices are arrived at by adding to the wholesale prices a marketing margin which covers overheads and a profit margin. The latter is markedly inferior to the one included in industrial prices, and does not exceed 2 to 3%.

The wish to guarantee the whole population a minimum standard of living, and to adjust supply to demand, is reflected in a fiscal policy which, depending on the individual case, increases or reduces prices. It can happen that products are sold at a loss. The commercial units concerned have their losses made good by a subsidy.

This rarely occurs on the home market, but there have been cases, such as that of scarce grains, where the prices paid to the communes were raised in order to stimulate production, or that of de luxe radio sets where the ex-factory purchase price was 495 yuan and the retail price was 400. When export products are sold abroad below the ex-factory price, the foreign trade companies are given a subsidy. As against this, a tax is added to the retail prices of certain products when demand exceeds supply.

The retail price policy would seem to be judiciously carried out, to judge by the absence of queues in China, especially if compared with the situation in other socialist countries. However, a partial explanation of the Chinese phenomenon is possibly to be found in the rationing of provisions and of certain industrial products. For grain, the rations are satisfactory – ranging from 11·5 kilograms a month for non-workers to 15 for employees and 26 for heavy workers.[1]

The adaptation of supply to demand is also affected by wage-control. It is remarkable that, even during the phases of marked economic expansion or of famine, no serious inflationary pressures have been recorded. The Chinese authorities have left enterprises free to dispose of only a small part of their profits – the amount paid into their welfare fund – and have kept wages stable. They have thus succeeded in keeping a strict control over the volume of money in circulation. They have also urged wage-earners to save to an extent which may appear surprising in a country in which incomes are relatively modest. In this way, national discipline underpins the policy of the Government.

The tendency of the Chinese authorities is to keep wages and prices as stable as possible. When rising production permits, they prefer to increase consumption by price reductions rather than by wage increases. Thus, according to press articles, the Government decided in 1970, in order to increase the peasants' standards of living, to reduce the price of industrial products for the countryside rather than to increase the prices at which grain was purchased. Nevertheless, in 1971, according to the China News Agency, the prices of certain agricultural commodities (other than those of the main cereals) were raised in the case of sugar beet by 15% and oil-seeds by 17%, in order to encourage their cultivation. Similarly, the

1. According to the figures supplied to foreign journalists in 1971 in Canton, the minimum ration is 15 kilograms.

prices of production requisites for agriculture were lowered – fertilisers by 10%, insecticides by 15%, kerosene by 21%, diesel oil by 10% and agricultural machinery by 16%.

The table below shows how cheap the basic necessities were in 1966, and prices do not appear to have changed much since then. If there has been a change, it seems to have been downward. A bicycle which was sold at 160 or 170 yuan in 1965 would nowadays cost only 140.

1966 prices in Peking (in yuan)
(one yuan = 0·41 US dollars at that time)

1 kilogram of wheat flour	0·32–0·36
1 kilogram of superior quality wheat flour	0·44
1 kilogram of rice	0·32–0·34
1 kilogram of superior quality rice ..	0·40
1 kilogram of sugar	1·40
1 kilogram of carp	1·80
1 kilogram of chicken	1·68
1 kilogram of duck	2·40
1 kilogram of pork	2·00
1 kilogram of cabbage	0·09
1 metre of cotton fabrics	1·50–1·80

1971 prices at Canton (in yuan)

Bicycle	140·00
Suit	8·00–9·00
Shoes	4·00
Watch	120·00
1 kilogram of rice	0·30
1 egg	0·10
1 kilogram of pork	4·00
1 kilogram of chicken	2·00
1 kilogram of carp	0·66

1969 prices in a brigade of a people's commune (Liuling)
(in yuan)
(according to Jan Myrdal and Gun Kessle)

Prices reduced since 1962 (1962 figures in parentheses)

Cotton tissue	0·84 (0·885) per metre
Rubber shoes	4·09 (4·59)
Mufflers	0·18 (0·435)
Vinegar	0·10 (0·18) per kilo
Earthenware jars containing 40 kilograms of grain	4·26 (9·91)
20-litre metal tins	5·30 (7·82)
Bicycles	145·00 (178·00)
Carts with bicycle wheels	100·00 (125·00)
Alarm clocks	7·10 (16·30)

Brandy, biscuits and sweets have also come down.

Prices increased since 1962

Sewing thread	0·18 (0·15) per reel
Oil	1·54 (1·44) per kilo

The State buys pigs at 50 to 60 yuan a piece.

The financial aspects of industrial enterprises

If industrial enterprises are allowed a certain degree of autonomy in running their business, they have no powers of decision as regards investments. Almost the whole of the enterprise's profits, if any, are transferred to the State. Any decision to carry out new investments is taken by the central planning bodies.

The enterprise is free to dispose of only a small part of the profits, in the form of a welfare fund which usually amounts to about 2% of the turnover. This fund is used for expenditures to promote the community's welfare and for improving working conditions.

But the bulk of the profits, which often represent 30% of the enterprise's turnover, and may be much more, are transferred to the State budget, 90% of whose receipts are derived from this source, including the turnover tax. An enterprise which has paid the State a high amount of profit may receive nothing back if the planner deems that it does not deserve priority – or, conversely, enterprises which make no profits or even incur losses may be allocated substantial financial resources if their production is regarded as having priority.

The enterprises are financed through the banking system. The funds earmarked for investment are placed at the enterprises' disposal by the 'Bank for Basic Construction'. These funds are not reimbursable, and bear no interest. This practice alone makes the calculation of cost prices completely meaningless. As against this, capital depreciation comes into the calculation. The working capital is formed by State contributions and bank loans.

Organisation of the enterprises before the Cultural Revolution

The organisation of industrial enterprises and the living conditions of people working in them were relatively well known before the cultural revolution, thanks to the reports of foreign visitors who were able to enter industrial establishments in fairly large numbers and question the directors, the engineers and the workers. Once the cultural revolution was over, the factories were thrown open again to foreigners, but visits are far less numerous than formerly, and the information collected is not easy to check.

At the head of the industrial enterprise is a director who is generally the man with whom foreign visitors have their discussions. He is as often as not a veteran of the revolutionary struggles, with his present post representing the party's reward. But the general policy of the enterprise is laid down by the factory party committee, which is elected by card-carrying factory members. The number of such members varies widely from one factory to another, but the party's guiding role in management is supreme. 'The system whereby responsibility is vested in a single chief, aiming at cancelling the party's guiding role', which was, it is alleged, the line recommended by Liu Shao-chi and his agents, was condemned and banned at the time of the cultural revolution. The factory manager is appointed by the supervising authority, which will be the technical minister in Peking or the provincial authorities. He is responsible for the day-to-day running of the enterprise, and must account for it to the party committee. In this way, collective direction and personal responsibility are combined in theory, but in this combination the election of the manager by the workers is ruled out. Those who, at the start of the cultural revolution, took the experience of the Paris Commune as their gospel thought again when they realised that the

43

Commune, during the short period in which it was able to work out its doctrine, recommended that the workers' assembly should elect the managers of enterprises and be able to dismiss them at any time.

The mass of non-party workers is not associated with the running of the enterprise, but it is frequently assembled in the factory for information and political indoctrination sessions. Its interests are defended by the trade unions, about whose degree of autonomy and influence little is known. No doubt they did not really understand the aspirations of the masses, for they were vigorously criticised during the cultural revolution.

A handicraft shoe factory in 1965

This factory is situated near a large town in a province in the interior. The premises are an irregular cluster of buildings, the main one being a large cement shed where most of the machines are housed. The factory employs 424 persons, including the manager and his cadres. Of these, 370 are men and 54 women. None of the workers is under 20. Twenty of them are lodged in the factory dormitories and in the factory itself, and the others live near by.

Wages run from 32·19 yuan a month for unskilled labourers (i.e. 386 yuan a year) to over 70 yuan (840 a year). At the canteen, three meals a day for six days a week costs them 8 to 9 yuan a month, i.e. just over 1 mao per meal (which is about 20% cheaper than in Peking).

This factory, which was established before 1949, closed down at the time of the liberation. The workers organised themselves in cooperatives but, as they had no tools, they had to rent them from the other factories. They were given a loan by the State for this purpose.

Since the liberation, the factory has never stopped increasing and improving its production. The output is at present 200,000 pairs of shoes a year (500 pairs a day, or just over one pair per worker) of which 45,000 are exported, mainly to Great Britain and the Soviet Union.

There is a fair range of models, which are robust rather than elegant. Three specialists are in charge of designing new models. The quality of production is good, and the local raw materials are famous.

The factory is entirely run on handicraft lines. All operations are carried out by hand without any use of power.

The turnover of the factory was 2·5 million in the year preceding our visit. The profits amounted to 18·4% of the turnover, and almost all of it was turned in to the State, i.e. 391,000 yuan. The factory retained 69,000 yuan for investment or amortisation. The other items of expenditure were raw materials (1,700,000 yuan) and wages (270,000 yuan, or 636 yuan per person on an average). The welfare fund which was used for old men and invalids as well as for recreation, education and welfare, was allocated 70,000 yuan, or a quarter of the wage bill.

The balance sheet shows a high rate of profit which mostly goes to the State. The amount of finance transferred to the State budget is over five times higher than the enterprise's investments. This ratio is particularly high, much more so than in the textile industry where it averages 2·4.

As will be seen, light industry was expected to supply substantial resources for national investment.

Wages

By virtue of their remuneration and living conditions, the workers in modern industries, as in all socialist regimes, form a privileged caste. It does not, however, seem that industrial wages have gone up since 1956, when they were raised by 14·5%, in line with the increase in productivity registered during the preceding years.

The scale of remuneration varies with the province, and sector. The highest paid are the coalminers and the lowest paid are in the textile industry. The average rate in the former is 80 yuan per worker, and in the latter, 55. Wage-earners are divided into eight categories, as is customary in socialist countries, and wages range from 36 yuan a month for the labourer who has just started work to 120 yuan for the most highly skilled workers, giving a smaller spread than in most socialist countries.[1] In exceptional circumstances, engineers of outstanding competence may be paid as much as 200 yuan, or even 300. On the other hand, a factory manager frequently earns less than the best paid worker. These figures go back to a point prior to the cultural revolution, but it is known that, at that time, Chinese economists were studying the possibility of reducing the spread by raising the lowest wages. It is not known what became of these plans, whose egalitarian stamp anticipated the doctrines of the cultural revolution, but, if we are to believe the figures collected during visits to factories during the summer of 1970, both wages and their spread are roughly the same as before 1966.

1. In a chemical factory near Peking, the gap between one category and the next was 6 yuan for the first six categories, where wages were 36, 42, 48, 54, 60 and 68 yuan respectively. The wage of the eighth category was 108 yuan.

The average wage (obtained by dividing the wage bill by the number of workers) seems to be from 55 to 65 yuan in the large factories. Since 1958, piece wages have been done away with, and remuneration is calculated monthly on the basis of the work norms per unit of time. There are forty-eight working hours in a week, i.e. eight hours a day for six days. There are no paid holidays in China, except for the workers and the cadres which have to work at some distance from their families. The only paid holidays are the feast days laid down by law, of which there are five. Workers are asked to put in overtime only in exceptional circumstances. These do not appear to be paid for.

Premiums were awarded over and above wages before the cultural revolution. Their very existence, as well as the question of profits, was at the heart of the debate on economism and material incentives. They formed a not insignificant proportion of the wage bill – from 7 to 17%, depending on the factory. Most of the workers were in receipt of them, but not the managers, engineers and employees. The rules governing the allocation of premiums varied with the enterprise. It seems that their distribution and amount were decided on by the workers' meetings on the basis of productivity, and also of the 'ideological conduct' of the recipients. Even before the cultural revolution, Chinese economists were loath to discuss this question and tended to play it down.

Premiums appear to have been done away with when the cultural revolution broke out, although in 1971 mention was made of them (apparently collective ones) to a foreign visitor in a factory in a large town. But it was never possible to obtain further details. The subject is a ticklish one, if only because premiums were condemned by the ethos of the cultural revolution. At the beginning of that movement, in 1966, factory managers were already avoiding the question. If some of them admitted that premiums were no longer being issued in cash, each of them had his own explanation of what had replaced them. If premiums have indeed been done away with by the cultural revolution, it would be interesting to know where the substantial resources freed by that decision have gone. Have they swollen the profits of the enterprises and been transferred, together with these, to the State budget, paid into the enterprise's welfare fund, or used to raise the lowest wages to reduce the gap between these and the highest wages? Whatever the truth of the matter, it will be seen that no foreign observer, even when he has been able to carry out his inquiry in China itself, can get to the heart of an issue which is of crucial importance to anyone wishing to understand how the economy works.

Standard of living of the workers

The standard of living of the workers in the modern industries is known to us in some detail from the information provided during visits to factories. The wages are supplemented by social benefits which, it seems, involve a deduction from wages of from 15 to 20%. This is a point which has never been cleared up in discussions with visitors. A full list is supplied of the social advantages granted the workers, but it is not explained whether part of their wages is deducted to cover their contributions. What is certain is that the enterprise bears part of the social cost of the social services through its welfare fund, which is replenished from the deduction of 2 to 3% of the turnover.

There are no family allowances, but the workers enjoy numerous social benefits – a pension of between 50 and 70% of their wage at retirement (which is 55 to 60 for men, and 45 to 50 for women); free medical attention for the sick and for expectant mothers, who draw 70 to 90% of their wages, and medical care at half cost for the members of workers' families.

The standard of living of Chinese workers in modern industry is far above the national average. To assess it correctly, one must not calculate it simply by converting the yuan, for the Chinese currency is manifestly undervalued. The real purchasing power of the yuan is much higher than would appear. The proof is that food in the canteens costs practically nothing by western standards. The bill is 9 to 15 yuan a month, depending on the region, for three meals a day, or about 70 meals a month. The average price of a meal is therefore 0·12 yuan, or five cents. Admittedly, the meals, though copious, are not very varied. They usually consist of a course of cereals with a little pork or fish. The cost of lodging, too, is extremely modest. For a rent which rarely exceeds 3 to 5 yuan a month, workers can obtain an apartment which may be small by western standards – 30 square metres for five persons – but seems spacious in a country where families are often crowded together in unhealthy premises with a living space of 2 to 3 square metres per person. In Peking, workers' accommodation costs 0·09 to 0·12 yuan the square metre per month. These prices enable the workers to put by some money, and foreign visitors are unfailingly informed that such savings – usually in State 4% bonds – are the general practice.

In these circumstances, it is not surprising that the workers in modern industries who are lodged in buildings put up since 1949 profess to be pleased with their lot, especially when they compare it with life as it was before the advent of the new regime.

Organisation of trade

Trade has for the most part been collectivised – at the same time as the other sectors of the economy. It is divided into a State sector and a cooperative sector.

The State sector has the lion's share, and, according to certain assessments, controls 80% of the volume of the wholesale trade and 60% of the retail trade. It is carried out by 'corporations' specialising in wholesale trading in the main categories of products. These trading companies conclude contracts with the industrial companies for the purchase of their output. They have ramifications at the provincial and *hsien* level, in the form of wholesale organisations which in their turn negotiate contracts with the enterprises.

The output of the factories is sold to wholesale depots by contracts stipulating amounts, qualities, prices and dates of delivery. These contracts are binding on both sides, and constitute an original feature of the Chinese system as compared with the more rigid system current in the other socialist countries.

Side by side with the State sector, there is a collectivised sector composed of selling and purchasing cooperatives which operate in the countryside, and which are said to run 30 to 40% of the retail trade. These cooperatives, whose number has been estimated at 30,000, are allocated the task of buying the agricultural output of the production teams on behalf of the State, and of selling to the rural consumers consumption goods which they procure either from the handicraft production cooperatives or from the trading organisations of the State sector. The director and personnel of the cooperatives are elected, and the members of the cooperatives share the profits. The cooperatives are grouped together in *hsien* and provincial federations and into a national Federation.

The cooperative concludes contracts with the production teams, collects and stocks the products thus purchased, and sells them back to the wholesale organisation in the state sector with a margin to cover its expenses. The cooperative can also buy the amounts produced by the teams over and above those stipulated in the contracts at the same price as that of the purchases effected on behalf of the wholesale organisations. It sells to the teams and the communes the necessary products for their agricultural labours – equipment, fertilisers and insecticides. Lastly, it runs the retail stores where members of the commune make their purchases of consumption goods, and which, as foreign visitors can see for themselves, are well stocked.

Private trade was reduced to a small percentage of the retail stores in 1958 after the collectivisation of the trade sector. It expanded again after the Great Leap Forward at the time when the family plots which had been abolished were restored and when greater initiative was left to private enterprise. It is possible that the cultural revolution gave it the final blow. On however modest a scale, private trading is regarded as an evil by the regime, for it smacks of capitalism.

Admittedly, it is easier to do without it in China than in other socialist countries where it has been done away with but the State sector is incapable of meeting the consumers' needs. For the distribution of both consumption goods and of services is well organised everywhere in China. The shops, once the serious shortages of 1959–1961 were overcome, are once again abundantly stocked. As all foreign visitors can testify, a wide variety of goods was to be had in the shops of the big cities in 1965 and 1966. Numerous well-patronised restaurants provided meals at moderate prices, thus confirming the high reputation of Chinese cooking. In every town there are stalls run by artisans and second-hand dealers, and shops of all kinds forming a sharp contrast with certain socialist countries. All foreign visitors have had occasion to appreciate the quality and rapidity of the service in the shops and restaurants, and the attentiveness and friendliness of the sales staff, worlds removed from the surly slowness and ill-will prevalent in many countries where trade is nationalised and where many of the employees in the State sector consider, as one of them has put it, that they are 'paid to work and not to work well'. In China, the affable welcome to clients in the shops is completely disinterested. The sales staff, who do not receive any premium on the turnover, have no material interest in giving the client good service or in persuading him to buy. They are impelled only by the desire to do a good job.

THE CHINESE ECONOMY

This picture of a well run country and an apparently satisfied population is still to be seen now that the cultural revolution is over. The shops are numerous and well supplied, and there is only one significant change from 1966: there are no more antique shops, except for one or two reserved for foreigners.

3. Population and employment

'How dense the population is', observed
Confucius while walking through the
land of Wei. He was asked what
could be done for it. 'Make it
rich', said Confucius. 'And when
it is richer?' 'Educate it.'

At the beginning of the regime, the Chinese Communist leaders believed – according to Mao Tse-tung – that 'a large population is a good thing for China, although it raises problems'. However, far-sighted economists such as Professor Ma, the rector of the University of Peking, warned of the dangers of too rapid an increase in population. A first birth-control campaign launched in 1956 ended in failure. It is only since the famine of 1960–61 that the Chinese leaders have realised the acuteness of the problem.

There is no need to elaborate on the serious disadvantages of a high rate of population increase in a developing country. It swells the number of useless mouths and the expenditure on food, clothing and education for the young, and reduces savings, and hence the rate of investment, whereas that rate should be as high as possible if the take-off to self-sustaining growth is to be achieved. Not only do infants and children cost the community dear without contributing anything, but they run the risk of not finding jobs when they reach working age, precisely because the cost of training them has proportionately reduced the investments indispensable for the creation of new jobs. Lastly, in agriculture overpopulation gives the maximum impetus to the law of diminishing returns on capital and labour.

The rate of population growth

There is little doubt as to the population objectives of the Chinese leaders, although those have never been officially announced. Economists have admitted in unofficial conversations that the rate of natural increase should be reduced to 1 % at the most, i.e. 10 per

51

1,000. Unfortunately, we know neither the actual rate of increase nor the effectiveness of the means employed to bring down the rate. Such official information as is available covers the period before 1958. The average annual excess of births over deaths is believed to have been 5 per thousand for the first half of the century. It rose to 20 to 25 per thousand during the First Five Year Plan. The birth rate had fallen slightly at that time – from 37 per thousand in 1952 to 32 per thousand in 1956 (which was the rate in the United Kingdom about 1890) and 34 per thousand in 1957 (the rate for Germany in 1900). It was then about halfway between the most prolific countries in the world (48 per thousand) and those for Europe and Japan. (Japan had 28 on the eve of the Second World War, 17·2 in 1957, 18·7 in 1966 and 19·3 in 1967.)

Improvements in public health had dramatically lowered the death rate. Whereas in 1933, according to very partial sample soundings, it was 34, it was only 18 in 1952 and 11 in 1957 – the same as that for the United States in 1958, and just above that for Japan (9 per thousand) and the USSR (8 per thousand). Its accuracy has been questioned on the grounds that the peasants made false declarations in order to obtain a larger share of land distributed when land reform was carried out. However that may be, this rate, which is comparable to that of most highly industrialised countries, can only be further reduced at the cost of heavy expenditure which China was and still is incapable of shouldering.

Progress in public health

The fact remains that the Chinese achievements in the field of public health have aroused the astonishment and admiration of eminent Western professors. In a short time, the new regime has set up a remarkably comprehensive organisation. The Academy of Medical Science, founded in 1957, comprises fourteen research institutes which employ 2,000 research workers and 4,000 technicians and administrators. In 1965, in addition to practitioners of traditional medicine, there were 150,000 trained doctors (who have an 8 years' course), assistant doctors (3 years) whose numbers were not known but were certainly greater than the fully trained doctors, and 170,000 sanitary assistants. The latter are given three or four months' training, and work for the greater part with the production teams in the communes. However, progress in hygiene is not equally marked in all parts of the country, and it was to remedy a lack of medical equipment in some regions that Chairman Mao coined the slogan at the time of the cultural revolution: 'Concentrate medical and sanitary work on the rural areas.' This led to the formation of teams of 'barefoot doctors' who were despatched to hospitals in the districts and communes.

Family planning

There is no doubt that an active birth-control propaganda campaign has been carried out the length and breadth of the country. The Chinese prefer to call it 'family planning', which has a less Malthusian ring about it. If foreign observers have sometimes doubted the existence of such a campaign this is because it does not use the press or the radio, or even posters, as the 1956 drive did. It may be that the Chinese authorities are anxious not to lose face after having had another burst of enthusiasm for a high birth rate during the Great Leap Forward, and are therefore careful to avoid visible forms of publicity. Perhaps also it is hoped that these more discreet means will prove more persuasive. In any case, it is known that the Chinese, on reaching the age at which they can have children, are subjected to oral propaganda by the party cadres and the administrative authorities during district, factory and commune meetings. They are advised not to marry too early, that is to say, not before thirty for the men and twenty-five for the girls, and not to have more than three children. The greatest pressure is brought to bear on young mothers after confinement. They are urged to space out births or to have no more children, depending on their housing conditions or their general situation. They are taught the usual birth-control techniques.[1] The more radical means (such as sterilisation of one of the spouses, or abortion) are available, but are never used without the consent of one of the spouses.

No information has so far been forthcoming from Chinese sources about the results of this campaign. It has almost certainly had considerable effects in the towns, for example in Shanghai, where the annual increase in the population was 1% in 1966, according to a statement made to foreign visitors by one of the deputy mayors of

---

1. Edgar Snow, speaking in February 1971, mentions the 'mass use of contraceptive pills'.

the town. The impact in the countryside may be slower and more problematic. Since 85% of the population live in agglomerations of under 2,000 inhabitants, the overall effect may be modest.

The examples of Hong Kong and Taiwan, it is true, show that a policy of birth control may be successful in a Chinese community. In Hong Kong, the birth rate dropped from 37·1 in 1960 to 24·6 in 1967, mainly because of the later age at marriage. In Taiwan, it fell from 39·5 in 1960 to 28·5 in 1967. But far less of the population in these territories is rural than in People's China.

While infanticide was practised in China (as in Japan) in order to adjust the population to resources, the Chinese have been taught, for thousands of years, to regard a large family as the secret of happiness. It would appear that they are finding it hard to break away from these accepted and traditional ideas, if the experiences of foreign visitors are to be believed. The director of a people's commune twenty kilometres from the centre of Canton, and hence within easy reach of the party directives and open to new ideas, has already had six children. He is over forty-five, and his wife is expecting a seventh child. When it was pointed out to him that such a large family was not in keeping with the government's policy, he merely replied: 'I like children.' In a people's commune near Shanghai, four women, all seemingly under thirty, were in the lying-in wards of the commune's hospital. A foreign visitor questioned them and learned that three of them were expecting their third child, and the other one her fourth. To conclude, let me quote the revealing parallelism between the growths in population and food supplies. In a commune fifteen kilometres from Chungking in April 1964, the director, when questioned about the increase in the commune's population since 1957, was hard put to it to reply, but he knew the number of inhabitants in these two years which showed an increase of 20%, and this was precisely the increase in food production.

It may be asked whether the authorities' efforts at persuasion will prevail over the lack of enthusiasm shown by the rural population to restrict births. Perhaps they will have to have recourse at some point to more draconian measures. So far, they have refrained from this, no doubt in order not to offend public opinion. In this connection, it should be pointed out that the 'punitive' measures which cut off food rations for any children after the third are fabrications of a propaganda hostile to the regime and adopted uncritically even by serious authors. All the Chinese questioned on this score denied the

existence of any such measures. On the contrary, there is no discrimination against the large families in the communes. In many
cases, the area of the private plot is proportionate to the size of the
family. In certain communes, there is an issue of cereals to which all
are entitled. It is allocated to each inhabitant regardless of age, and is
made *before* the issue based on the work carried out.

What is the present population of China?

The present population figure is not known even by the Chinese
leaders, if we are to believe the statement made by Chairman Mao to
Edgar Snow in December 1964. Mao was unable to reply to this
question and merely observed that 'he did not believe that the
Chinese population was as high as 680 or 690 million, as some people
in China affirmed'. Are we to conclude that, by affecting ignorance
on this question, Mao was avoiding the issue and observing the rule
of secrecy imposed on all Chinese? The explanation given by
Chairman Mao of his ignorance was even more disconcerting. The
peasants, he said, did not report deaths, because they were anxious
to hold on to the clothing rations of the deceased. If peasants are able
to avoid reporting deaths, this can only mean that they enjoy the
complicity of the whole people's commune, including the leaders.
Clearly, then, the official population statistics published for the
decade 1951–60 must be treated with the greatest reserve.

The reliability of the 1953 census has been questioned. This is the
only one to have been carried out in China by the Communist
regime, or, more exactly, the only one where the results have been
published, for the possibility cannot be excluded that other censuses,
on a more limited scale, have been taken which have not been made
public. According to this census, which took a long time to complete since it was published only in November 1954 but apparently
used modern techniques, the population of Mainland China was
582 million at 30 June 1953, plus 7,591,000 in the island of Taiwan.
Foreign observers are divided as to the veracity of the former figure,
which is higher than the estimates made before 1949 suggested.
Some consider the figure as being from 3 to 15% below the real
population, and, in that case, the population was between 613 and
685 million as early as 1953. Others believe that the return was
deliberately inflated by the Peking leaders.

750 million – at the most – in 1970

Depending on which figures are selected for 1953 and the rate of increase since then, the number of inhabitants in 1970 is somewhere between 750 and 850 million. The lower hypothesis seems more probable, since it is difficult to see how agriculture, whose output up to 1970 had not come up to expectations, could feed 850 million inhabitants. Nearly all observers believe that the 1969 production of cereals was not more than 15% above the 185 million tons harvested in 1957, and hence that it is in the order of 210 million tons on the most optimistic hypothesis. Unless it is supposed that the *per capita* consumption has dropped, which is improbable, for it is close to the basic minimum, it is not clear how a harvest of 210 million tons could feed a population of 850 million, even if we add in the five million-odd tons imported every year. On this hypothesis, then, the *per capita* availability would be only 235 kilograms, as compared with 300 kilograms in 1957. These are only crude figures. Klatt put the net consumption of cereals at 170 kilograms *per capita* in 1966, which gives 1,650 calories. This figure is definitely lower than that for the USSR, which in 1966, according to Soviet sources, was 3,000 calories. The 450 calories which are added to the 1,650 from cereals are provided by vegetables and soya (150), fats and oils (120), meat and poultry (80), fruits and vegetables (60), sugar (20) and eggs and fish (20). The 2,100 to 2,200 calories *per capita* available in China may be regarded as sufficient, taking account of the climate and the productivity of labour.

The most probable figure for the 1970 population is therefore 750 million. This tallies exactly with Mao's estimate in 1964 which was below 680 million, to which must be added, if the rate of increase is put at 2% a year since that time, over 80 million inhabitants.

As to the figure of 700 million, which is given in the statements by official personalities and is quoted in the Peking papers, it is merely an approximation which is felt to be appropriate to the subject being discussed, and which every so often is modified so as to bring it into line with the growth of population. It was for a long time 650 million. Soon it will be raised to 750 million.

Population forecasts

Any forecast as to the population in 1980 or 2000 is in the nature of a guess, for neither the present population nor the rate of increase is known with any degree of certainty. The spread in 1985, for example, may be from 860 to 1,300 million, depending on the hypothesis adopted. What is certain is that China's development will be closely connected with the size of its population at that date. If, as may be expected, the rate of increase can soon be reduced to 1%,[1] the Chinese population may not be over 900 million in 1985. This forecast may seem on the conservative side, but it is substantiated by the statement in 1966 by a Chinese economist to a foreign journalist: 'The increase in China's population is not nearly as great as is claimed in capitalist countries!'

Employment problems

The population figure is not the only one that interests economists. A knowledge of the age pyramid is also of capital importance for employment forecasts. The 1953 census was too hasty to provide much useful information on this score. However, the increase in the birth rate registered since 1950, thanks to the peace and to the improvement in public health measures, has certainly led to a substantial increase in the working population from 1968 on, if this is taken to include both those over 18 and also younger people, given that working life begins before 18 in a country where secondary education is still only accessible to a minority.

Whatever the effect of the birth-control campaigns, whether past or future, and whatever the rate of population increase in the coming decades, the country is already facing the problem of finding employment for the age groups born after 1949 and now coming on the labour market in increasing numbers. This is a new situation for China, since, up till 1968, only the age groups born before 1950 were reaching working age, and, since food supplies were precarious and public health poor at that time, the rate of infantile mortality was high. The rate of increase in the working population may therefore be put at less than 1% up till 1963.

The problem will become particularly acute throughout the 1970s. The working population has been increasing since 1963 by over 2% a year. It can be estimated that, from 1968 on, the age groups

1. In a statement to the Canadian Minister for Foreign Trade in July 1971, Chou En-lai confirmed the Chinese Government's intention of reducing the rate of population increase to 1%. He added 'that if the rate fell below that figure, so much the better'.

reaching working age will be from about 20 million to 25 million. The age groups who can opt for retirement will be much less numerous, so that from 10 to 15 million new jobs will have to be created every year for young men and women if they are not to be underemployed in the country. But, according to plausible estimates, the number of new urban jobs does not exceed 500,000 a year. From 1980, on the contrary, there will be a dip in the numbers of new recruits to the labour market, reflecting the drop in the birth rate and the increase in infantile mortality during the three famine years of 1960 to 1962.

It is fairly obvious that Chinese leaders and planners have only recently woken up to the gravity of the problem. The First Five Year Plan should have enlightened them. The rate of investment was high, and the rise in production was remarkable. Yet employment did not increase in the same proportion. The greater output was in fact due more to an improvement in productivity than to an increase in the number of people employed.

The leadership has from the first set its face against the rural exodus which was threatening to flood the towns with an unwanted excess of manpower. It is not surprising, once civil order was restored, that rural populations with a very low standard of living should be attracted, as in every country in the world, to the towns. On the 7 September 1966 the Minister of Agriculture, Tanchenlin, announced, according to the *Red Flag of Science and Technology* (6 March 1967): 'Everyone wants to go to the towns. There a man can earn 30 to 40 yuan a month just by sweeping the streets, whereas in the country he can earn no more than 200 to 300 yuan a year, or 20 yuan a month. Among those present here, who are there who would voluntarily become peasants?'

China, unlike most other developing countries, vigorously opposed this flight and moved many of the immigrants back to their place of origin. In the five years covered by the First Plan, they succeeded in limiting the number of rural emigrants to 8 million[1] and the increase in urban population to 7% (or, according to certain other writers, to 30% – from 71 to 92 million). However, this moderate increase was

1. It was probably in part this desire to check the flight from the country which led to the introduction of food rationing in 1956 at a time when agriculture was admittedly in a bad way. Food tickets were only valid for a particular town, and any changes of residence as between towns, or a move into a town, could be easily controlled by the authorities.

still a serious matter, since it was not possible to meet the towns' increased needs or to avoid inflation.

It was the realisation of the increasing overpopulation of the countryside which was one of the decisive factors in the Great Leap Forward. Jobs had to be found for the masses of underemployed, not to say unemployed. The following years convinced the leaders even more strongly of the need to keep the increase in the urban population down to the lowest possible levels, for otherwise it would be difficult to feed them. 'Until agriculture is mechanised,' said Po I Po, at that time one of the key figures in planning, 'the urban population must be brought down from 130 to 110 million inhabitants.' But agriculture at present needs extra hands only for the seasonal peaks.

The cultural revolution was accompanied by fresh migrations to the towns and villages. From 1966 to 1970, one million inhabitants out of ten seem to have left Shanghai, especially young graduates, officials and party cadres. It was to employ this extra manpower in particular that the campaign was launched to stimulate ancillary activities. Traditionally, a high proportion of rural income is drawn from this source. For the time being, the creation of small industries constitutes the only means of creating a large number of jobs for the young people coming on to the labour market. This policy was imposed in 1960 by the inadequacy of financial resources, and was based on strategic imperatives after the deterioration of relations with the USSR. It was in line with the need not to leave young people to rot in semi-idleness in the countryside when they could not be offered jobs in the towns.

But the most serious aspect of the employment problem is the lack of outlets for those who have taken their higher school or university certificates. All developing nations have grasped the capital importance of the need to spread education if productivity is to be raised. It is here that the socialist countries have achieved their greatest successes. As long as China had a rapid industrial expansion, that is up to 1960, the demand for cadres of all kinds was greater than the supply. Workers had therefore to be trained on the job and given tasks normally performed by skilled manpower. The First Plan was accompanied by an extensive programme of education, and the secondary schools began to train the necessary cadres.

From 1960 on, the general provision of primary education generated an inflation in the number of pupils attending secondary and higher institutions. Millions of college graduates – from 3·6 to 6 million according to certain estimates – were turned out by secondary and higher institutions from 1950 to 1960. They had no difficulty in finding work in the secondary and tertiary sectors,[1] where there was a shortage of cadres. From 1960 to 1966, the situation had changed radically. The labour market was flooded with 23 million college graduates at a time when the stagnation in industrial investment, especially in large-scale industry, was sharply reducing demand.

Most of these graduates were aware of what they owed to the new regime, which had given them the chance to complete their education. Many of them were the sons of poor or middle peasants who were encouraged to pursue secondary studies for ideological reasons. The children of middle-class parents, who were losing their majority in the universities and were somewhat suspect politically, were on the contrary allowed to continue their studies only if they were specifically gifted.

Some of the young graduates – the best of them – were taken on to replace the hastily improvised cadres trained under the First Plan. But most of them, once they had left their schools and universities, could not find a job in the towns and were sent back to the country. The role played by these young people in the Red Guards disguised the real problem for a time. The fact was that all of them could not find work in the people's communes. Other outlets had to be created. And here, as despatches of the Chinese agencies since 1969 have emphasised, many of the young secondary school graduates were enrolled in the 'Production and Construction Units'. These units, created in 1953, were for some time restricted to Sinkiang, where they developed 660,000 hectares of land and founded a hundred or so State farms. Since 1969, analogous units are believed to have been set up in other frontier regions. Their total numbers are about 600,000 in Sinkiang, 300,000 in the Autonomous Region of Mongolia, 200,000 in Heilungkiang (part of former Manchuria) and over 100,000 in Chinghai and Tibet. Their objective is to people the desert regions, develop their agriculture and to provide military reserves on the frontier with the USSR which could reinforce the army and the militia.

1. The secondary sector refers to manufacturing, the tertiary covers services (Translator's note).

Distribution of population by sector

If the population increases considerably every year, there does not appear to be any marked change in the proportions of the employment sectors. In 1957, according to official statistics, 72% of the population was engaged in agriculture, 16 to 17% in the secondary sector and 11 to 12% in the tertiary sector. The Great Leap Forward entailed decisive changes, but the situation reverted to the *status quo* shortly after.

The urban working population – in agglomerations of over 2,000 – has been relatively stable since then at 50 million. It was estimated at from 40 to 60 million in 1957.

Of this total, a third is engaged in industry and handicrafts.[1] The number of wage-earners in modern industry is unlikely to exceed ten million or so out of a working population of some 400 million. A not insignificant proportion of this ten million is female – almost 20% in 1959, even in heavy industry, while many men who would like to work in these industries are unable to find a job in the towns. This situation has a specifically political explanation. The regime is proud of having changed the status of women in a country where up to 1911 they were definitely regarded as inferior. It regards the access of women to industrial jobs, even exhausting ones, as illustrating the dignity which it has conferred on them. The other reason for the extent of female employment in industry is economic. The allocation of jobs in factories to married women and girls reduces the number of homes in towns, and the cost of community investment, especially in housing, is thereby cut. Female employment in towns has had interesting effects. By allowing many homes to earn a double salary, it has increased still further the gap in the standard of living between town and country, especially since the wages of female workers in industry are exactly equal to those of male workers. In the communes, on the contrary, payment is by output, so that males, being more robust, usually come off better.

Another consequence of women's employment in the towns is that the parents leave their children with the grandparents whose influence is not usually favourable to the new ideas. The 'old customs' and the 'old conceptions', which were spurned by the cultural revolution, therefore survive and flourish.

1. The official Chinese statistics do not distinguish between these two types of activity, which in any case merge into one another.

61

4. Agriculture

*The riches of a nation depend not
on the number of its inhabitants
but on the amount of food at its
disposal.*

Han Fei-tse
(*philosopher of the
school of the legists,
who died in* 233 B.C.)

Some twenty years after the initiation of a planning policy which for ten years gave heavy industry priority, agriculture still has an important place in the economy. Although, as Chou En-lai has stated, its share in the gross national product has dropped since 1949, when it was about 50%, to almost 25%, it still provides two-thirds of the nation's jobs – according to a Chinese economist speaking in 1966, who put the number of peasant homes at 120 million, distributed over 600,000 villages. At the end of the regime's first decade, about 85% of the population still lived in agglomerations of less than 2,000 inhabitants.[1] In 1949, the figure was 89·5%.

Agriculture also provides half of China's exports by value, or indeed two-thirds, if account is taken of the raw materials used in the textiles exported. Agricultural imports, even now that these include 4 to 5 million tons of cereals a year, do not nearly equal the exports in value.

The preconditions for agricultural development are not, on the whole, very favourable. According to Chou En-lai, speaking in 1966, the cultivated area is only 108 million hectares,[2] that is, 11·4% of the total area. Admittedly, there is double, and even triple, cropping on at least 20 to 30% of this area. A considerable proportion of the cultivated land is under permanent irrigation – 20 million hectares

1. This refers to the rural population, which is to be distinguished from agricultural population.
2. The lack of certainty about the most fundamental data on the Chinese economy is illustrated by the fact that, if we are to believe the writer, Han Suyin, the figure for the area cultivated, mentioned by a Chinese economist (also in 1966), is 120 million hectares.

in 1932; 34·3 in 1957; and perhaps 40 at the present time out of a maximum irrigable area estimated at 80 million hectares.

The density of rural population is one of the highest in the world. The cultivated surface is 1,400 to 1,600 square metres per inhabitant – the uncertainty being due to the absence of a firm figure for the population – and 1,800 square metres per person in the countryside. If in this respect China is not so well off as India (2,350 square metres per inhabitant in 1967) and Pakistan (1,850 square metres in 1967), it is better off than Japan (600 square metres per inhabitant but 2,100 square metres per person living in the rural areas).[1] In the early stages of Japanese economic development, i.e. between 1868 and 1900, the cultivated surface per inhabitant was 1,600 square metres. Japan, it is true, is favoured by a climate with a regular rainfall, which shields it from serious drought, while at the same time the fact that there are no large rivers means that it is spared the floods which frequently devastate the countries on the Asian continent. In China, the extensive irrigation works undertaken did not succeed in bringing under control the natural disasters of the years 1959–61. These, according to the official versions, were the worst for a century in a country which has suffered twenty-one major floods from 1901 to 1966. In 1964 and 1965, years in which the country should have registered marked progress in its harvest, the North was still badly hit by drought, and production in that part of the country was only fair.

The quality of Chinese soils is not particularly good. A study in the *Jen Min Jih Pao* (*People's Daily*), dated October 1959, divided them into 31% fertile, 40% ordinary and 29% poor. The loess soils are fertile, but they are in regions where the rainfall is very unequal. Many Chinese soils seem to have lost much of their original fertility. It is estimated that 75% are deficient in nitrogen, 60% in phosphate and 20% in potassium.

The Chinese peasant had reached a point where he was extracting from his land the maximum yield possible without the help of modern technology. His productivity, other things being equal, was comparable with the best in the world.

The USSR had founded its industrial power by forcing agriculture to subsidise the economy. But Russian agriculture did not suffer

1. As early as 1766, according to Cressey, the cultivated surface of China per inhabitant was only 2,170 square metres, as compared with 3,500 in 1661 and 7,200 in 1578.

63

from the Asian problem of overpopulation, and the level of *per capita* income enabled the country to draw on the agricultural surpluses to finance industrialisation. In China there were practically no surpluses, and the leaders could not treat the peasants as harshly as the Soviets did. The Chinese revolution was carried out by a peasant army, and it is inconceivable that a regime which owed its power to the peasants could milk them dry. On the contrary, the avowed intention of the Government is to reduce the disparity between the standard of living of the peasants and the workers. That explains the relative elasticity of Chinese policy as regards agriculture. Even when China looked to the Soviet development model, i.e. up to 1958, it never tried to finance industrial development by making agricultural incomes pay 'tribute', to use Stalin's expression in 1928.

It is significant that the 'middle' Chinese peasants were never liquidated 'as a class' like their opposite numbers in the USSR, the kulaks. On the contrary, Government policy was aimed towards their integration. Mao Tse-tung was himself the son of a peasant of this class who owned at least a hectare, and also dealt in grain, and he was never disposed to underrate their enterprise and talents. When, in 1955, he saw for himself in his journey through China that land reform had not done away with peasant inequalities, and that a new class of rich peasants was being formed, he did not deport them as Stalin had done, but sought to absorb them into socialist cooperatives.

True, the equality of which Mao had dreamed has not yet been realised among the peasantry. It may seem astonishing that, after years of collective ownership of the land and the means of production, people still speak of the 'peasant classes' and that a distinction is made, as it was under the Kuomintang, between poor, lower middle, upper middle and rich peasants – whereas the expression 'poor peasants' has long ago disappeared from the Soviet vocabulary. The reason for this was revealed by the Red Guard papers during the cultural revolution when discussing the divergencies within the central party committee, from 1961 on. The moderates wished to fix the quotas for the delivery of agricultural products to the State on the basis of the family, while the radicals were opposed to this, as they feared, with some reason, that this path would lead them back to the private division of the land, even though such a distribution would be carried out equally among the families.

There were apparently deals among the peasants about the plots, whose area was at that time sometimes raised to the equivalent of a third of the team's land. Moreover some peasants increased their plots by clearing land on their own behalf. Other factors making for inequalities between families were the development of secondary activities and the possibility of selling produce on the free market.

The persistence of these types of class behaviour explains why, even before the cultural revolution, the regime never ceased to warn the poor and middle peasants of the dangers of a return to capitalism, and urged them to be unremitting in conducting the class struggle. We do not know to what extent these appeals were heeded in the rural areas. Their very frequency and their dramatic character seem to indicate that this was no mere rhetorical exercise designed to stimulate vigilance, but the reflection of a genuine fear on the part of the authorities. The result was doubtless an atmosphere of suspicion which undermined the spirit of solidarity in the communes' work, and created tensions which may be one of the factors responsible for the poor showing in agriculture. However, it is vital not to underestimate the importance of this class struggle in the rural areas. The regime depends above all on the poor and lower middle peasants. Even so, the cultural revolution, despite its appeals to carry on the class struggle, does not seem to have caused disturbances in the countryside.

Flexibility of agricultural policy

The socialist transformation of agriculture was carried out more rapidly than the leaders themselves had envisaged. No doubt the pace of collectivisation reflects Mao Tse-tung's desire to put a prompt end to the supremacy of the rich peasants resulting from the first land distribution. But it is also possible that these precipitate changes upset the countryside and are the real reason for the difficulties experienced by agriculture.

Once the collectivisation of the land was completed, i.e. in 1957, it might have been thought that the Chinese authorities would call at least a temporary halt. There was therefore general surprise, particularly among the Soviet experts, when it was learned (in August 1958) that it had been decided to move at one leap from a collective regime of the *kolkhoz* type to an institution unprecedented in the history of socialism – the people's commune, 'of grandiose historical significance' . . . 'as fresh as the rising sun on the vast horizon of

C

East Asia' (as various Chinese publications put it). Conceived as the basic unit for all aspects of social life – economic, cultural, administrative and military – the commune was the owner of all goods, exercised general competence in economic management, and merged with the administrative jurisdiction in which it was situated, the *hsiang*. It was to be the laboratory of a communal life, preparing the way for the transition from the socialist to the Communist system.

It is hardly necessary to repeat that this institution, in its most ambitious concept, did not survive the Great Leap Forward and that, even if it still survives, it is in a much modified form. The people's commune, except perhaps in certain extreme cases, was never the kind of barracks in which, as some journalists have alleged, the peasants were regimented, fed in canteens and lodged in dormitories. But even the commentators most favourable to the regime recognise that the Chinese economy was not sufficiently advanced to move on to collectivisation in the form of the people's commune. The production relations which the Great Leap Forward wished to establish were, to use the Marxist terminology, in advance of the development of the productive forces. In the long run, however, the Chinese leaders are determined to make the people's commune the basic institution of the agricultural economy.

People's commune of Malo in the Shanghai suburb (1966)

This is one of the communes most frequently visited by foreigners.
It is near the most populous city of China (10,400,000 inhabitants) and enjoys many advantages (guaranteed outlets for the most expensive produce, high investments, fertile land, etc.).

It certainly does not represent the average Chinese commune, but a visit to it is instructive in many ways, in view of the pains taken by the director to reply to questions.

History of the commune. In 1950, about 5,000 families were living on the territory at present occupied by the commune. In the first stage of collectivisation, 647 mutual assistance teams were formed, but there were disagreements between them on the question of crop rotation.

After the constitution of semi-socialist cooperatives in 1955, 30% of the income was distributed in proportion to the work performed. Finally, the peasant owners were persuaded to forego the ownership of their land, and 10 socialist cooperatives were formed. In 1958, they were merged into a people's commune with 14 brigades and 147 teams.

At present, the commune has 5,670 families and 25,180 inhabitants, or an average of 4·4 per family. This figure seems low, but it is much the same in almost all the communes visited by foreigners. Out of 25,180 inhabitants, 12,000 work, which suggests that the figure includes almost all the men and women.

The area of the commune is 3,200 hectares, of which 2,263 are planted out to rice, wheat, maize and cotton.

Crop yields:

Average yield of all cereals
1949	38 quintals per hectare
1957	51 quintals per hectare
1965	111 quintals per hectare

Rice yield for a single harvest: 75·11 quintals per hectare
Yield of winter rice: 33 quintals per hectare (May harvest)

Cotton yield
1949	97 kilograms per hectare
1957	315 kilograms per hectare
1965	930 kilograms per hectare

The cotton in question is almost certainly ginned cotton, for this figure is definitely lower than that for other communes visited by foreigners (2,025 kilograms per hectare of seed cotton). These figures seem exaggerated to experts who, from a study of fields before picking, have assessed yields at about 1,500 kilograms.

Use of fertilisers: 400 kilograms of chemical fertiliser per hectare, with a fertiliser content of 25%, to which must be added an unspecified amount of natural fertiliser.

Number of pigs
1949	4,000
1957	8,120
1965	34,100

partly communal and partly raised on the family plots.

Distributed income from communal agricultural activities:

154 yuan per inhabitant per annum
300 yuan on an average per working person, or a 197% increase
    over 1957, when it was therefore 100 yuan.

Educational establishments of the commune. In 1957, the commune had six primary schools attended by 620 pupils, and in 1965 24 primary and six secondary schools with over 5,000 pupils, or 20% of the total population. One hundred and fifty-five children of the commune are studying at university level institutions in the towns. (Education, like the police, is financed by the State, whose contribution seems to be deducted from taxes.)

There are 10 handicraft workshops, of which six are run by the commune and four by the brigades. Only members of the commune are employed, in these workshops, without any outside labour, and they produce ploughing implements (harrows, rice-husking tools), wickerwork, pasta from beans, Turkish towels, and chemical fertilisers and oil-cake. They are also engaged in woodworking and in processing cereals.

Income from these ancillary activities constitutes a useful addition to the commune's earnings. A part of the workshops' output is sold outside the commune.

Financial accounts of the commune:

Receipts
Overall value of the communal production
(agriculture and cattle-raising),
excluding ancillary activities   7,190,000 yuan

Expenditure
Working expenses	2,157,000 yuan or 30%
Administrative expenses	28,760 yuan or 0·4%
Taxes paid to the State	294,790 yuan or 4·0%
Capital and welfare funds	798,090 yuan or 11·1%
Remuneration of commune workers	3,918,550 yuan or 54·5%

Income from family plots. The area allocated to private cultivation is one-tenth of a *mu*, i.e. 66 square metres per person, and that of the family plot is proportionate to the number of persons in the family, or (on an average) 290 square metres per family.

No statistics for the income from family plots are kept by the commune, but they can be put at 15 to 20% of the communal agricultural income distributed, that is, at from 25 to 30 yuan *per capita* and per annum, and from 110 to 140 yuan per family.

Agricultural collectivisation since the Great Leap Forward

The communes still exist, but they are smaller, and their number has risen from 24,000 to 74,000. They may still comprise as many as a hundred villages. Their jurisdiction in most cases is confined to such matters as schooling (which, contrary to what some people have written, is not always free since educational supplies are often a charge on the parents), medicine, police and the people's militia.

They are run by a director appointed by the party and assisted by a management committee chosen by the conference of representatives, who are themselves elected by all the members of the commune. The communes retain the ownership of communal equipment such as the handicraft workshops, tractors, lorries and cooperative stores. The brigades, too, which number about ten per commune, own certain production implements.

But the nucleus round which work on the land is organised is now the 'team', which generally corresponds to a village. It is this team which, in the framework of the general planning directives, can determine how the land is to be developed and fix the objectives and methods. It is the team that signs the contracts for the purchase of the production requisites (fertilisers, seeds and insecticides) with the trading corporations, and also the contracts for the sale of their produce. Lastly, it is among the members of the team that the income from the common effort, whether in cash or kind, is distributed.

As can easily be imagined, distribution raises difficult problems. Peasants are not wage-earners like the workers on state farms. Income depends on the volume of overall output. This means that a bad harvest is reflected in a fall in income. However, distribution is proportionate to the work put in, and the hardest working and most efficient workers receive a higher share than those whose weaker physique or lack of enthusiasm for work leads to a lower output.

The difficulty lies in making a fair estimate of the work put in by each member. The original system was one of *basic points*, which paid for work by time units, and took account of the worker's skill. But this was a crude system and made no allowance for the quality of the work.

Work norms were then applied. Each task was remunerated by a certain number of work points in terms of the norm set for that task. The norms were fixed by the members of the team, and the work put in by each was subjected to a check every evening. The accountant who carried out this check could be elected by the members of the team.

Original methods of remuneration have been worked out by certain communities in line with the policy of the central authorities of leaving the initiative with the masses. The Tachai brigade, in the loess soils of Shansi not far from the Yellow River, is the regime's proudest symbol in this connection, and is held up as a model to the rest of the country. Thousands of visitors, Chinese and foreign, have already visited it.

The Tachai commune has realised that the most serious disadvantages of the work points system are the complicated way of calculating them, the time needed to apply them, and the feeling of some members of the team that their work has not been well enough remunerated. The commune considers that it has found a way round these difficulties by giving the workers themselves the responsibility of recording their own efforts. Under this system, reliance is placed on the judgment and honesty of each member. Various agricultural jobs which can be accomplished in a day are allocated work points proportionate to the difficulties. Once his day is done, the peasant allocates to himself the number of points he thinks he has deserved by comparing the work he has done with the jobs listed in the classification.

Remuneration is not the only problem facing the communes. The inequality of peasant incomes as between one production unit and the other worries the regime's theorists. The income distributed, for equal work, varies widely with the regions and even, inside the same region, within the commune, and indeed within the team. When this inequality is due, not to the difference in the work put in, but to natural conditions, it is unjust and therefore contrary to socialist ethics. Should a peasant farming a sterile plot of land in a community afflicted by natural disasters be paid less than one who has not made a greater effort but has been favoured by the fertility of the region? Chinese economists who have reflected on the land rent[1] have not so far come up with an answer.

The distribution of income between the peasants is effected partly in kind, in the form of husked rice or flour, and partly in cash, especially by means of the resources derived from compulsory sales to the State. The income distributed among the members of the team is of course the net income after deduction from the gross income of the sums earmarked for taxes, the capital and welfare funds, and the working expenses which cover mainly purchases of seeds, fertilisers and insecticides.

1. The land rent represents, in Ricardo's economic theory, the proportion of output in agriculture due to land, as opposed to the parts due to labour and capital.

To start with, the agricultural tax was calculated as a percentage of a national income, as is the case in France for the land tax. This income was fixed for a five-year period, but it does not seem to have been modified at the end of that period. The tax forms a diminishing percentage of real income where the value of output is increasing. This type of fiscal policy favours the most productive teams, since they pay the same tax every year, irrespective of the value of their output. The higher a team's output, the lower the percentage of tax it has to pay. In the rich communes, the tax corresponded to some 4 to 5% of the communal income on the eve of the cultural revolution. This percentage is considerably less than that of the tax paid by the Soviet *kolkhozes*, but the latter have higher incomes than the Chinese people's communes.

In the rich communes near the large towns, the tax represents under 30% of what may be considered as the gross profits. In that case, 70% of the profits are left to the commune to form the capital and welfare funds, whereas in industry the factories are obliged to transfer the whole of their profits to the State, and the only financial resources they receive are for their investments, provided these are in the State Plan. The communes' autonomy in the matter of investment is one of the essential features of government policy.

In the USSR, under the Stalinist regime, the bulk of the finance skimmed off agriculture was obtained by operating the price mechanism. Agricultural produce was bought from the *kolkhoz* farmers at very low prices, sometimes below cost, and sold by the State in the towns at far higher prices. In China, it seems that the margin between the price paid to the team for cereals and the price charged to urban consumers is no higher than the real costs. Husked rice (ordinary quality), which is paid for at 1 mao 21 fen a pound[1] to the producer, is sold for 1 mao 60 fen a pound on the Peking markets. The margin of 40 fen represents a third of the purchase price, which seems to correspond to the transport, processing, storage and distribution costs. The price of agricultural products paid to the producers does not appear to have risen since 1956 except for some coarse cereals.

Part of the income is earmarked for the capital and welfare funds, and varies with the wealth of the communes and the weather. However, there may be some evening out of the differences between the teams within a commune by a grant to the less well off, but, up to the

1. The yuan is divided into 10 maos and 100 fen.

present time, nothing has been done to palliate inequalities as between one region and another.

The favoured position of the peasants in the matter of financial autonomy clearly entails some risk. If the party and the planning authorities are not careful, the majority of the peasants in a commune may prefer to increase consumption at the expense of investment. And in fact, if we are to believe recent press statements, not all the communes are disposed to earmark substantial sums for the investments needed to set up small industries.

The net income, i.e. the income distributed to the workers after deduction of taxes, working expenses, and the amounts allocated for the capital and welfare funds, varies from 45 to 60% of gross income. It is not surprising that, in such a vast and varied country, peasants' incomes may have as wide a spread as from 1 to 12. In the communes visited by foreigners (which are not located in the poorest regions), the income per working person averages from 200 to 600 yuan, although the higher figure is quite exceptional. If it is remembered that a family usually includes two working persons, the income resulting from the sharing out of the communal income is from 400 to 1,200 yuan per family. But foreign journalists have visited communes in the far south where the income per worker was only 50 yuan a year.

To this income from the community must be added a figure for the private family plots. The area allocated for this purpose had risen before the cultural revolution to a maximum of 7% of the area cultivated by a team – and not 5% as certain writers have reported. The plot is smaller in regions with a high density of population, such as Kwangtung, than in those which are remote from the large towns. Its area is at times proportionate to the number in the family, which proves, as we have seen, that the policy of birth control has not been carried to the point of penalising large families. This family garden may cover from 30 to 300 square metres which the peasant is free to work as he wishes. In most cases, he raises pigs on it (one or two per plot which he can sell to the State for 50 or 60 yuan each), poultry, rabbits and geese. In the south, one can find tobacco and sugar cane as well. It is difficult to put a figure on the income from these plots. It is not taxed in any way, or included in statistics. The plots constitute a departure from socialism and are regarded as a survival from capitalism. Hence, questions on the subject by visitors elicit only laconic and evasive replies. Chinese economists, even before the cultural revolution, went on record as favouring the experimental suppression of these plots in pilot communes[1] and ultimately their complete disappearance. They added that their existence was less and less justifiable as the agricultural situation improved and the communal income increased. However, the income from this source is far from negligible. It is believed to amount on an average to 15% of the communal income, and has even been put as high as 30% in a commune visited by foreigners.

Recent visits to China show that the plots have survived the cultural revolution, but it appears that they have sometimes been reduced out of respect for the current ideology. In any case, this is a subject which is passed over in silence by the press and the radio. If the private strips have been spared, this seems to be because the peasants cling to them and would strongly resent their abolition.

The peasants supplement their income from the land by ancillary activities traditional in a country where rural overpopulation condemns a large part of the agricultural labour force to idleness during the slack season. From time immemorial, these occupations have allowed the Chinese peasants to manufacture most of the objects of current consumption which they need. These occupations are still justified, in part because of the inability of the urban industries to meet all the population's needs for manufactures, and partly because of the importance of keeping a diligent and competent labour force busy. A number of these handicrafts find an outlet abroad, and are an appreciable source of foreign exchange for a country which has no great surpluses to export.

The ancillary activities may be private or communal. If they are private, the income goes to the family. This is the case with embroidery and wickerwork, the gathering of medicinal herbs, or the collection of water fleas on the surface of ponds. But most of them are communal, and, in that case, they are paid for within the team, as are most types of farming work, according to a scale of work points. The workshops of the people's communes manufacture small industrial and agricultural items such as buckets, pasta and Turkish towels. In a commune in the neighbourhood of Shanghai, people in the workshops are paid like industrial workers. They earn 30 to 40 yuan a month, i.e. 420 yuan a year, whereas the average income of the peasants in that commune is 300 yuan. Far from declining, these

1. Even before the cultural revolution, the private plots had been suppressed in certain communes, for example, in Tachai – the model case.

activities have been given encouragement by the authorities since the Great Leap Forward. It has been realised that, in view of the shortage of resources, China cannot in the near future hope to build up a modern industry rapidly. The authorities have therefore decided to promote the emergence and development of small rural industries. These industries have the advantage of needing much less capital from the State than the large modern plants, and can do without the heavy social investments called for by new industries in the towns. They provide supplies of equipment and production goods to the rural areas. They offer employment to a constantly increasing population, and in particular they make it possible to employ most of the younger people who, on completing their education, have not found a job in the towns. There has thus been a return to the concept which inspired the Great Leap Forward – use the surplus rural manpower to industrialise the countryside. These establishments are often constructed with whatever comes to hand, are supplied with poor quality raw materials (and fairly irregularly at that), and turn out wares of varying quality. They may therefore have a low level of productivity. No matter. It is better to make whatever use is possible of the surplus manpower than to leave it idle and disgruntled. This rural industrialisation, which, carried to excess, led to the setbacks under the Great Leap Forward because it was launched without sufficient preparation, will prove fully justified if it is implemented with discrimination, as long as China does not have the capital to create new jobs in the towns.

The peasants working in these small factories make the most of the industrial equipment and raw material available. A number of communes are now capable of constructing agricultural equipment, and even small electric generators. Others have the equipment needed to process agricultural commodities such as sugar, wheat and rice. It is planned to encourage the communes to manufacture preserves.

This industrial decentralisation on a nationwide scale was inaugurated in 1957, when a large number of industrial enterprises were transferred from the State Ministries in Peking to provincial or municipal bodies. At the present time, this tendency seems to be gathering momentum. A new industrial model is thus emerging which is adapted to the country's conditions and derives the maximum benefit from its resources. The lesson of the Great Leap Forward has been learned. This time, local industrialisation is not being carried through by 'forced marches' as it was to some extent in 1958. Greater care is being taken to ensure that the supply of raw materials and equipment to the decentralised production units is soundly organised.

A people's commune in the Canton area in 1964

Since the cultural revolution, visits by foreigners to communes became few and far between, though they are now being resumed. The following account was published by the *Neue Zürcher Zeitung* in January 1970.

The people's commune which was visited, probably as a result of the autumn Canton Fair (15 October–15 November) was that of Ping-Chou, near the provincial capital. It has 64,000 inhabitants and 14,000 families, or just over 4½ persons per family – the usual number noted during visits to people's communes whatever the province, which seems low in a country regarded as 'overpopulated' . . .

The commune is formed of 17 production brigades – or just over 820 homes per brigade – and 275 production teams.

The cultivated area is 4,600 hectares, or 7/100 hectares (700 square metres) per person. Four thousand hectares are planted out to rice, and the rest to sugar cane, vegetables and fruit.

The private plots cover only 3% of the total area of the commune, that is, 138 hectares for 14,000 families, or 100 square metres on which a family can raise one or two pigs and a dozen hens. Any produce from the plot not consumed by the family must be sold to the commune, and not (as was allowed before the cultural revolution) on the free market. There are 70,000 pigs on the territory of the commune, of which 50,000 belong to it and 20,000 are raised on the family plots, giving an average of a pig and a half per family. In addition to providing meat, the pigs supply manure for the soil, as they have traditionally always done.

Mechanisation is still on a modest scale. The commune possesses only 24 used tractors which allow it to cultivate 230 hectares out of a total of 4,600 belonging to the commune.

The yield of the rice crop was 92 quintals[1] a hectare in 1969 – probably with double or triple cropping, but the writer of this account is not specific on this point – which is an exceptionally high figure, since the average Chinese rice yield is put at 27 quintals. Before the liberation, the yield was 34 quintals a hectare. The harvest amounted to 41,000 tons, which does not tally with the two previously mentioned figures of 4,000 hectares of rice with a yield of 92 quintals, giving a production of only 36,000 tons. (No doubt, this discrepancy can be

1. A quintal is a tenth of a metric ton, or 100 kilograms.

attributed to uncertainty about the area cultivated which was put at 4,000 hectares by the spokesman of the commune, whereas it is in fact 4,400.) This confusion in the figures given to visitors is a frequent occurrence, but it is not certain whether it is due to the spokesman or to the interpreter, who is always fallible. The rice production in this case is therefore 640 kilograms per person per annum, and the consumption is 416 kilograms per person per annum, or 35 kilograms per month – a quantity distinctly higher than townspeople's food rations.

The wages (paid in two instalments) of members of the commune are, on an average, 156 yuan per person (presumably to be interpreted as person employed, although that is not specified). To this, there must be added the wages in kind – 300 kilograms of rice a year, some oil, four metres of cotton fabrics, and fuel for the homes.

The article reports certain points made by the spokesman of the commune. Mechanisation is still insufficient. The commune is not rich enough to effect a substantial rise in its members' standard of living: productivity is very unequal as between the brigades; some produce 120 quintals per hectare and others 75. It was not explained whether these inequalities were due to the difference in the fertility of the soil or in the farmers' skill or industriousness.

In concluding his account, the spokesman made the standard comment that the commune must in the main 'rely on its own strength' if it wished to expand production.

In any case, the peasants' standard of living is much lower than that of the urban workers. It is only in some very rich communes that the annual *per capita* income of the working population is as high as 400 yuan, and yet that is hardly as much as a labourer earns in the towns when he starts work in a factory. The average income of a peasant throughout China is probably less than 150 yuan per working person, whereas that of the workers in the town factories, who are admittedly only a small proportion of the population, is about 700 yuan a year. On the other hand, life in the country is easier since provisions cost 30 % less than in town, being distributed directly by the team to its members without any charge for transport, storage, processing and marketing. Lodging is generally free. (Every peasant is the owner of his house.) So are fuel and water. Lastly, the peasant can supplement his income by ancillary activities on his family plot or at home.

The most remarkable results have so far been registered in these few communes which are well equipped with the means of production. There are as yet, however, only a few of these, as can be shown by calculating China's potential yield from the 108 million cultivable hectares if this yield were equal to those of the Malo people's commune at Shanghai or of the Sino-Albanian Friendship commune at Peking. To take only rice, which is grown on about 30 million hectares, the production would be 255 million tons, whereas, in 1969, it was less than 120 million. The interesting point about these spearhead communes is that they show the kind of yields which agriculture can obtain when it is given adequate production requisites. When the Government can make available to the peasants sufficient quantities of fertilisers, insecticides and agricultural equipment, it will be easy for them to feed the population, even if it continues to increase rapidly. The progress achieved between 1960 and 1970 in the production of fertilisers and equipment may be expected to continue in the seventies. What is more, a new development may completely transform the agricultural situation. It ought to be possible to adapt to Chinese conditions the high-yielding varieties of rice (and other cereals) which have been so successful in India and the Philippines. There is complete silence on this point in China, but experiments are being carried out on these varieties in selected people's communes. Imports of IR 8 seeds, which can give a yield of as much as 65 quintals per hectare per crop, are said to have been brought in via Pakistan and Nepal. It remains to be seen how long it will take for these varieties to be disseminated among all the communes.

Technical means of improving output

However much the Marxist leaders rely on collectivisation, they realise that agriculture can only make further advances if supplied with modern production requisites. Up to 1960, following the Soviet model, the Chinese gave priority to industry in the allocation of their investment. In the First Plan period, agriculture received only 7·6% of overall investment. However, a 12-year agricultural development programme was worked out for 1956 to 1967 parallel with the Five Year Plan for the economy as a whole. The targets of this Plan for 1967, if compared with the actual production figures, show up the wide gap between ambitions and achievements. If we confine ourselves to the cereal crop, we see that, according to the Programme, it might be 360 to 380 million tons in 1967 which, it was explained, 'with 500 kilograms *per capita*, should make it possible to meet the minimum food needs of the population'. The final objective of the Programme was even to guarantee, in the subsequent years, a ration of 750 kilograms *per capita*. However, in 1967, which was an excellent year, the harvest, according to optimistic estimates, was only 230 million tons.

It is worth setting out the twelve points on which, according to the Programme, the modernisation of agriculture was to concentrate:

1 Hydraulic works: irrigation and flood control
2 Increase in production of natural and chemical fertilisers
3 Improvement of traditional implements; expansion of mechanisation
4 Development and dissemination of seeds adapted to local conditions
5 Extension of area under double cropping
6 Increase in area under high yielding crops
7 Improvement of crop patterns according to local needs
8 Improvement in productivity and use of soil
9 Flood control and soil conservation
10 Increase in number of draught animals
11 Fight against insects and plant parasites
12 Development of fallow lands to increase cultivated area

Priority has always been given to irrigation works in China which, in view of the climate, have always been of the greatest importance. Foreign visitors throughout history have been struck by the vast extent of the hydraulic works in this country. From 1952 on, new works were started. Then, during the Great Leap Forward, an exceptional effort was made which is estimated to have involved 50 billion hours of work from 1959 to 1960, or 960 times the labour needed to dig the Suez Canal. Large dams were built. One of them, the equivalent of the Serre-Ponçon dam in France, took less than a year, using 40,000 workers. This 'human investment' was not achieved without some setbacks, owing to the lack of preparatory studies which, in any case, were usually bungled. From 1960, no mention has been made in the press of large dams, but irrigation works are pushed ahead unremittingly. In 1966, numerous press articles were devoted to the construction of large canals in the Tientsin region, and, more recently, to development works in the Hai basin which were carried out with 260,000 workers on an area of 265,000 square kilometres, and in the Huai basin (the Huai is a tributary flowing in from the left to the Yangtse Kiang) where 200,000 workers dug a 130-kilometre canal and built a number of dams.

Terracing and levelling works continue. The tenacity of the peasants of Tachai in this respect is extolled. They are obliged to exercise constant vigilance, for the torrential rains wash away the terraces, and force them to reconstruct them again and again. Earth-levelling is carried out in the whole of the country. It is an unspectacular but profitable operation which consists in preparing the soil over millions of hectares in order to make irrigation possible.

Reafforestation is indispensable in this country where trees have usually been overexploited. Millions of hectares have been replanted, with differing results depending on the care devoted to the new plantations, but on the whole successfully. René Dumont, however, has noted certain errors in their methods of establishing new plantations of fruit trees.

But whatever the truth of the matter, these vast operations have transformed the Chinese landscape, and in particular the great northern plains.

Mechanisation

Mechanisation does not, for the time being, have the same meaning in China as in Europe and America. It is not a question of the spread of mechanical traction, or of the introduction of machinery in order to save manpower and carry out agricultural tasks at the most favourable moment and in the shortest time. Conditions are different from those in the USSR, a land of plains with a sparse agricultural population and extensive cultivation where manpower is inadequate and is spread over a huge cultivated area twice as large as China's.

The mechanisation of Chinese agriculture takes less spectacular forms. Wheelbarrows and carts with tyred wheels tend to replace human carriers. Semi-mechanised appliances, which are gradually substituted for traditional implements, make possible deeper ploughing, closer sowing and more careful harrowing and weeding. Diesel and electric pumps are gradually replacing waterwheels driven by foot which still form part of the rural landscape. All this equipment is being supplied to the peasants in increasing numbers. But it is still far from sufficient, and only a third of the irrigated land is watered by pumps.

Tractors are still few and far between, and they are a rare sight even on the broad northern plains. Some of the rich communes on the outskirts of the big cities have them, but most of the existing tractors are used in the sparsely peopled regions in the northwest or northeast where most of the State farms are to be found. In 1968, the rolling stock of tractors was under 150,000. Some of this was imported from the Communist countries and the balance was from Chinese factories. The best known of these is the one at Loyang, which is believed to turn out 10,000 a year. It is a good indication of China's priorities at the present time that the main importations of transport are lorries and locomotives, not tractors. The use of tractors is unlikely to become general in the near future, and mechanisation in China will, for a long time to come, consist essentially of the supply to the peasants of irrigation equipment and implements.

Chemical fertilisers

After having followed the Soviet example of the Thirties and neglected the production of fertilisers, the Chinese leaders realised, after the Great Leap Forward, that they needed to guard against further famines, and accordingly gave priority to supplying the countryside with chemical fertilisers. The Chinese peasant has long fertilised his land with vegetable matter, mud from the marshes, animal manure, and, above all, human manure. China's main objective, at the time of the First Five Year Plan, was to become an industrial power as rapidly as possible. It did not therefore feel that any special effort was needed to develop agriculture, and it relied mainly on the application of traditional methods by its peasants to increase production. But the experience of the Great Leap Forward showed that agriculture was exposed to disturbing lapses, and that neither the collectivist structures nor human investment in large infrastructure operations were adequate substitutes for modern production requisites.

The target in the Twelve Year Plan (1956–67), which had been fixed in 1962 at 3 million tons of fertilisers, was raised to 6 million tons in 1957 and to 15 in 1967. The priority given, from 1961 on, to the production of fertilisers did not lead to the construction of large production units like the one at Nanking, which has 18,000 workers, or Tai-Yuan, which was begun in 1958 with Soviet assistance and which produces several hundred thousand tons of ammonium nitrate a year. China did not possess the necessary technical and financial resources to construct the equipment, particularly the compressors needed for large units. Most of the increase of production had to come from small nitrogen plants scattered all over the country. Offices with specialised knowledge about the production of fertilisers were set up in all the administrative areas. Small factories mushroomed, and they numbered over a hundred by 1966. Whereas in 1961 their combined output was only 2% of the national total, in 1966 it was put at 800,000 to 900,000 tons, or an average of 8,000 tons a factory. A more recent figure credits them with 40% of total production. A new model of converter has been developed by engineers in a Szechwan factory, working in collaboration with researchers at Peking University.

European businessmen attending the Canton Fair in May 1970 visited a people's commune where they were shown a small liquid ammoniac factory with a capacity of 5,000 tons a year. The commune, which also had at its disposal a quarry and a lime kiln, was self-sufficient in fertilisers. This is the only example of its kind shown to foreigners in recent times, and there is no means of knowing whether other communes are in such a favourable position. In any case, it is one of the declared objectives of the government to see that the communes become self-sufficient as regards fertilisers.

The production of nitrogen phosphates has also increased, especially in the hilly southern regions, where there are phosphate deposits such that the raw material has merely to be crushed to be ready for use as fertiliser.

The total production of fertilisers appears to have marked a 15% increase in 1966 over 1955, and, according to unofficial Chinese sources, to have reached the level of 8 to 9 million tons compared with 631,000 tons of nitrogen fertilisers in 1957. These figures have been questioned as overoptimistic. What is fairly clear is that China is still far behind Japan in the use of fertiliser per cultivated unit. The content of nutritive elements in chemical fertiliser used in China has been put by one writer at 8 kilograms per hectare.

The priority accorded to fertilisers for agriculture is confirmed by the growing volume of imports which supplement domestic production. The main supplier is Japan, whose f.o.b. prices are higher than those of European producers but whose freight costs are much less. From 2 million tons in 1967, Chinese purchases of Japanese fertilisers have risen to 2,250,000 tons in 1968 and 3,200,000 tons in

1969. The cultural revolution did not hamper the rise in these imports, as was the case with other products which were regarded as less essential for the economy. European sales are lower than those of Japan, but they too have increased – from 111,000 tons in 1964–65 to 751,000 tons in 1968–69. The demand by China is for ammonium sulphate, urea and ammonium nitrate. This choice illustrates a cautious attitude. But if the Chinese are hesitant about buying high-content ammonium nitrates, which are the most effective, this is no doubt because the sudden expansion in the use of fertilisers in recent years has not been without its failures. Due to a lack of competent assistance from the extension services, certain production units have had unfortunate experiences with chemical fertilisers. As a result, the Chinese authorities do not make new types of fertilisers available to the communes before having carried out lengthy trials on pilot farms and experimental plots. It will be noted, moreover, that the amounts of compound fertilisers purchased are very small, and those of potash fertilisers are nil. It would appear that fertilisers are applied preferably to industrial crops – cotton, soya, sugar and tobacco.

In February 1971, Chou En-lai told Edgar Snow that there had been a very marked increase in fertiliser production since 1966, and that it had come close to 14 million tons in 1970. If we add the 4 million tons of imports, consumption seems to have exceeded 160 kilograms of commercial fertiliser per hectare, or about a sixth of Japanese consumption. Can it be increased substantially in the next few years? This is a complex question. It is doubtful whether imports can be stepped up much further in view of the modest foreign exchange reserves. The expansion of domestic production will depend not only on the small plants, which have a capacity of some 10,000 tons a year, but also on the big factories of the type constructed during the Great Leap Forward. In order to facilitate development on the latter lines, China is seeking to acquire the necessary technical knowledge from abroad. In the years preceding the cultural revolution, China ordered two large factories – one from a British company for ammonia, and the other from a Dutch company (which has constructed it in Szechwan) for urea with a capacity of 500 tons a day and at a cost of 5·6 million dollars. Chinese engineers ought now to be in a position to build factories of the same type.

If China makes do with a third as much fertiliser per hectare as Japan, Chou En-lai considers this consumption target can be reached by 1975, which presupposes roughly a doubling of the present level.

The cultivated areas

The extension of the cultivated area may seem to offset the density of the rural population in a country where only 11·4% of the land is farmed. This has not, it is true, been the case in Japan, where the percentage of cultivated land – which is 16% – has not changed for a century except in the northern island of Hokkaido. The First Five Year Plan envisaged an expansion in China's cultivated area of 2·6 million hectares. The Twelve Year Agricultural Programme (1956–67) put at 6·7 million the number of hectares to be developed by 1967.

Officially the figure of 100 million hectares has been mentioned as the area to be opened up, which would double the present figure, but it is fairly clear that this question has never been seriously examined. In 1956, the additional land suitable for development was scaled down to only 43 million hectares. The Soviet experience with the virgin lands in Asia has taught the Chinese leaders to be cautious. In marginal lands with a harsh climate, setbacks are almost inevitable. In any case, the investments needed would be crushing and far beyond China's resources, in tractors alone.

The peasants are attached to their native soil and are not at all keen to emigrate. They have only done so when density of population has become intolerable. The settlement and development of Manchuria, for example, was the work of peasants from Shantung – a province on the southern shore of the Pechili Gulf which was all that divided them from their new home. But even today northeast China (formerly Manchuria) is sparsely populated as compared to the rest of the country, and has only about 80 million inhabitants in its million square kilometres. Although the Manchu emperors forbade the Chinese to emigrate to that area, there was a clandestine immigration into it from 1850 on. Crop yields are still low, and it is significant that the Chinese press announced, for the first time in 1966, that they had shown a considerable improvement. However, no transfer of peasants to northeast China has been organised by the Communist Government to ease pressure on the more densely populated regions.

The opening up of new lands is usually effected by State farms. Although analogous to the *sovkhoz*, they do not play the same part in the Chinese economy. The Chinese have never, like the Soviets, proclaimed that the realisation of socialism would at some point involve the transformation of the *kolkhoz* into a *sovkhoz*.[1] They do not aim at transforming the peasants into State wage-earners. While the Soviet *sovkhoz* cover some 20 million hectares out of a cultivated area of 200 million, the area of the Chinese State farms is only 5·5 million hectares out of 108 million. The most recent figures available date from 1961. According to them, there were then 2,940 State farms in China – as against 710 in 1957 – which covered 5·5 million hectares and employed 2·8 million workers (or, on an average, 5,000 square metres per worker and 860 hectares per farm). Most of the land occupied by the State farms is on the Soviet frontier – in the northeast and Sinkiang – or in the south. In the latter area, they are often peopled by overseas Chinese. A Ministry for State Farms and the Opening up of New Lands was created in 1956. We know little about these farms, which are rarely mentioned by the Chinese press and are not open to foreign visitors.

According to Edgar Snow, 12 million additional hectares were opened up from 1960 to 1970. New sources of food have also been acquired by the cultivation both of land on the embankments separating the fields (which have been rendered superfluous by collectivisation) and the land surrounding the ancestors' tombs which, in the Shanghai area, disappeared only at the time of the cultural revolution. However, these leaders do not look to other land to increase production. They do not covet territory in Siberia, for example the maritime provinces with their mild climate, in order to settle them, and they do not lay claim to them as 'living space'. These areas do not have the attraction for them that Manchuria did for the Japanese, cooped up as they were on islands with no raw materials. What China lacks is not agricultural space. She has more than twice as much per peasant as Japan. It is the means to increase productivity. The frontier claims of the Government of Peking are not prompted by the unavowed plan to extend its territory and settle the new land with surplus population. Other considerations, such as *amour-propre* and political expediency, have led to the denunciation of the 'unequal treaties' which established China's frontiers with Russia.

1. Admittedly, the Soviet leaders have had second thoughts. They no longer call for the extension of the *sovkhoz* at the expense of the *kolkhoz*.

Agronomic research and extension of modern methods

Agronomic research, which was almost non-existent in 1949, was given a tremendous fillip at the time of the Great Leap Forward. The Academy of Agricultural Science, founded in 1957, is the equivalent of the agronomic research centre at Rothamsted in England. It has good standards but its staff of research workers is still inadequate to meet its needs. In 1964 an Agronomic Institute for the use of nuclear radiation was opened. Work is carried out on radio elements, calcium, strontium, phosphorus and sulphur, which indicates the existence of an advanced atomic industry. The Institute has a good supply of cobalt for such work of up to 5,000 curies, and the appropriate television equipment.

In addition to the national research institutes, there is a network of district institutes subordinate to the Academy which carry out research and, above all, experiments in thousands of fields ranging from one *mu* (one-fifteenth of a hectare, or 666 square metres) to 20,000 hectares.

On the whole, the means available are still modest, and Chinese agronomic research is too inexperienced to meet the country's needs and attain an international level for another ten or twenty years.

One of the less costly means of raising productivity in agriculture is the popularisation and dissemination of modern techniques. But it was immensely difficult to teach vast numbers of men, for the most part illiterate, poor and habit-ridden, methods so utterly different from those practised by their ancestors and handed down from generation to generation. Ignorance and distrust did not make things easier. And, to complicate matters even further, a large number of the 120 million peasant homes were in relatively inaccessible areas.

The regime, from the outset, proclaimed its resolve to teach the peasants new and more effective farming methods. It implemented this policy by campaigns against illiteracy and by extension drives, but it was hampered in these initiatives by lack of resources and of trained cadres at all levels.

The diffusion of new techniques has been effected by multiplying experimental fields, explanatory campaigns, the training of medium and lower cadres, and their despatch to the rural areas of agronomic students. The authorities appear to have been careful not to force these new methods on the peasants, but to introduce them

85

gradually, except perhaps during the Great Leap Forward. They were at pains to win over the old peasants, whose experience was valuable and whose support was indispensable to success. Thereby, by a seeming paradox and a very Chinese compromise, they bowed to tradition and harnessed the wisdom of age to the adoption of the new methods. However, quite a few errors were committed by cadres whose zeal outran their competence. But, on the whole, the education of the masses is slowly paving the way for better methods. It is characteristic that one of the directives for the cultural revolution in the countryside called for priority in the spread of a practical knowledge of agriculture. Lastly, the periods spent by students and intellectuals in the country (which are justified on ideological grounds) have the advantage of easing the shortage of cadres – accountants, mechanics and instructors.

The volume of agricultural output

In a country where the development of the whole economy depends on the level of agricultural production, the volume of the harvests forms the basic datum for anyone wishing to assess the state of the economy. The estimates of the harvests by foreign experts are very approximate, and differ widely. They are based mainly on the weather bulletins which are issued by the provincial wireless stations and by the local and national press. But we are only imperfectly informed of the increases in yields due to the stepping up of investments and to technical progress.

For the year 1969, the estimates of harvests vary from 190 to 210 million tons, according to the source – American, Japanese, Soviet or Hong Kong Chinese. These figures are equivalent to those for 1967, which were from 190 to 218 million – and even 230 million. Of all these estimates, those of Professor Ishikawa for the years 1952, 1956–57 and 1965 appear to be the most accurate. (See table on opposite page.)

It emerges from these tables that *per capita* consumption of cereals increased in about the same proportion as the population. This is an impressive achievement. The assumption is confirmed by the fact that food rations were, it appears, the same in 1970 as in 1957. The constant level of imports since 1961, the year in which they began, seems to attest the stability of the food situation in that field. If there had been any deterioration, the Peking government would

Balance Sheet of Cereals
including sweet potatoes and soya beans

In millions of tons	1952	1956/7	1965
Total resources			
National production	163·913	192·720	207·5
exports	0·468	2·325	1·0
imports	0·021	0·190	5·7
Fluctuations in stocks		3·160	
Total	163·466	193·747	212·2
Details of total			
Seeds	9·300	10·100	10·050
Food for animals	20·104	27·400	29·010
Food industry and breweries	3·784	4·945	5·240
Human food	130·278	151·300	167·900
(Loss in processing last item estimated at 19·1%)			
Consumption per capita	185kg	194 kg	191 kg
Net consumption is therefore	105·395	122·402	135·840
	(567 million inhabitants)	(628 million inhabitants)	(707 million inhabitants)

have increased them by drawing on its foreign exchange reserves or by transferring foreign exchange earmarked for other imports.

It must not be forgotten that, if cereals provide the bulk of the calories consumed by the Chinese, these are supplemented by other foods, vegetables, fruits, meat, fish and fats for example, the production of which appears to have increased more rapidly than cereals since 1952. The population has adequate rations of cereals, and tends to seek to improve its diet by increasing its consumption of other foods.

Main agricultural products

The distribution of production between the main cereals is as difficult to establish as the total volume of the harvest. The most commonly cultivated cereal is rice. Chinese agronomists tend to regard rice as more important than other crops with which they are less familiar. This crop is spreading north. In 1957, it covered 32·3 million hectares, or 30% of the cultivated area, with an average yield of 27 quintals per hectare – taking account of double and triple cropping – as against 40 to 50 quintals per hectare per harvest in Japan where double cropping is the exception, and 50 to 60 quintals in the Democratic Republic of North Vietnam in 1970. In the more fertile regions of Kwangtung, yields were as high as 60 to 70 quintals of paddy rice per annum. Western experts have ascertained, for example, that, in a commune with double cropping, the yield per harvest was 30 quintals of paddy rice, rising to peaks of 50 quintals, whereas the director of the commune affirmed that it was above 45 quintals.

The production of wheat, although increasing, is far from being comparable with that of rice. This cereal is cultivated on an area only 15% smaller than rice but has generally only a very low yield – 11 quintals per hectare.

The main industrial crop is cotton, the production of which is enough for the needs of a population which, even in the north, hardly uses anything but cotton fabrics. The average yield of cotton is probably not more than a ton per hectare, which is substantially less than the Soviet figure (2 tons per hectare).

Cattle-raising has never been on any great scale in this country where the plains are overpopulated and the hills poorly farmed, or used for terraced crops. Animals compete with men for food. The south has only the buffalo, which is used for ploughing the ricefields, and the north has only draught animals.

The existence of millions of natural pastures (300 million hectares, according to some writers) which are still practically underdeveloped holds out considerable scope for cattle-raising. It is doubtful, however, whether they can be exploited in the near future because of the lack of the necessary skills and experience.

Balance sheet for agriculture in 1970

Until the record cereal crop in 1970, which was over 240 million tons (or 16% over 1969), some doubt was possible about agriculture's ability both to feed the population and to contribute to the expansion of the economy. China was continuing to import cereals at the rate of 2 to 3% of its needs. Its agricultural exports, which form its main source of foreign exchange, had for the most part been stagnating for years. In 1966, a Chinese economist recognised that yields were lower in his country than in Japan, and that China's agricultural production was not as high as America's, although that country's population was less than a third of China's. The production of cereals was merely keeping pace with the population, though other commodities were being produced much faster, e.g. pork and vegetables. All this despite the fact that the labour force in agriculture was increasing, since the natural increase of the rural population was not absorbed by the flight to the towns.

Moreover agriculture had had the benefit for ten years of the infrastructure operations begun under the Great Leap Forward, and also of increased supplies of fertilisers, insecticides and agricultural equipment. Only the sector using modern production requisites appeared to be progressing, but it covered only a small proportion of the cultivated area.

The explanations of this state of affairs differed according to the ideology of the observer. Advocates of a liberal economy attributed it to the collectivist system itself. They noted that agriculture was the weak spot of the socialist economies in Europe, and deduced that things could not be different in China, and that the relatively meagre results obtained were due to the faults of the system. The insufficiency of material incentives and the apathy of the peasants were sufficient to explain the situation. The peasants devoted all their efforts, they argued, to cultivating the family plot, where yields were alleged to be much higher than those from the communal lands on which their efforts were half-hearted. Their lack of enthusiasm, said these writers, explained the State propaganda machine's insistence on the need for harder work, and the emphasis attached to the stimulating example of Tachai. The bulk of the peasants had turned a deaf ear to these appeals, and, since they were now assured of a basic minimum, showed no sign of increasing their productivity.

Those who were thus putting the Communist regime in the dock alleged that *per capita* food availabilities were lower than in 1933. But there was no statistical apparatus at that time, and in any case their reasoning is based solely on arithmetic means. It glosses over, too, a number of aspects of the pre-1949 situation – the marked inequality between the various classes of society, the indebtedness of most of the peasants, and the regime's inability to come to the help of the regions hit by natural disasters which are so frequent in China.

In fact collectivisation and efficiency are much less incompatible in Chinese agriculture than in that of the European socialist countries. In China there has always been a bond between peasant owners, and a tradition of collective effort born of the need to operate irrigation systems, the battle with disasters, and the high density of the rural population. China therefore was better prepared for life in a collectivist regime. Moreover, the vast majority of farmers before 1949 – 70%, it appears – had no land of their own, or only a tiny patch, as two-thirds of the land was in the hands of the big land-owners and rich peasants. The land reform carried out by the Communist regime initially involved distribution to the landless, but the resulting system did not last long enough for them to become attached to private property, since in 1955 all peasants were called upon to form cooperatives of a more advanced type, to which they had to contribute their land. In any case, it seems debatable whether collectivisation alone can be held responsible for the modest agricultural output. Even hostile authors recognise that, given the techniques at present employed and the degree of the fertility of the soil, the yield from the land is as high as it could be. This means that in modern China agricultural output depends less on how the farms are run than on improvements in technology. The leaders have realised this, since they have not carried collectivisation to its logical conclusion by abolishing the family plots, even during the cultural revolution, and have concentrated on increasing the necessary production requisites.

Production of Cereals[1] in China
(millions of tons)

1957	1958	1964	1965	1966	1967	1968	1969	1970	1971
185[2]	200[3]	190–200	185–207	180–206	190–230	180–206	210	240	246

1. The official Chinese statistics for cereals include potatoes, which are counted at a quarter of their weight. The potato harvest can be put at 25 million tons. From the figures in the table above, we must therefore deduct the figure of 6·25 to obtain the weight of cereals properly so called.
2. The last year for which official statistics are reasonably reliable.
3. For 1958, the official figures were 375 million, amended to 250 million, which is also an overestimate.
   The cereal harvest appears to be distributed as follows:

rice	45–50%
wheat	15%
other cereals	30%
potatoes	5–10%

Agriculture's relatively poor performance till around 1970 has puzzled those agronomists who had followed the considerable improvements in farming conditions by the regime. In 1965, René Dumont confessed his perplexity when he compared the low yields with the generous investments effected during the previous seven years. He advanced the hypothesis that the land, cultivated so intensely for centuries without periods of fallow, but admittedly with constant applications of natural fertiliser which reconstitute the organic elements, had gradually lost its original fertility. In the same way, there has for some time been a process of salinisation and alkalinisation in many places in the north which it is difficult to combat. It is not impossible that the excesses of the Great Leap Forward upset the delicate natural equilibrium maintained for century after century by the peasants.

By 1970 the position had changed. The figure for the production of cereals in that year attests that the regime is reaping the benefit of its earlier investments.

The New China Press Agency announced on 22 December 1970 that the cereal and cotton crops had been a record. The cereal crop,

Imports of Cereals by China
(millions of tons)

Country of origin	1966	1967	1968	1969	1970	1971
Argentina	1·580	—	—	—	—	—
Australia	1·445	2·700	1·620	(2·200)	—	—
Canada	2·695	1·508	2·200	(1·450)	—	—
France	0·109	—	0·584	(0·800)	—	—
	5·820	4·208	4·404	4·450	3·2	3·2[1]

[1] Forecast

n.b. Account must be taken, in drawing up the balance sheet of foreign trade in cereals, of Chinese rice exports (about 1 million tons a year, not including supplies to the Democratic Republic of North Vietnam).

It may also be recalled that China imported rice from 1933 to 1937 at the rate of 800,000 tons, and that, during the first decade of the Communist regime, it did not import wheat and *did* export rice (500,000 tons in 1957; 1,200,000 in 1958 and 1,500,000 in 1959, excluding aid to Vietnam).

according to Chou En-lai, was 240 million tons, an increase of 32% over 1957. The prime minister mentioned, in addition, the existence of 40 million tons of reserve stocks scattered throughout the country in small silos or in the peasants' own barns. The spread of the new high-yielding varieties has contributed to this progress. So has the extension of irrigation and flood control, which is indispensable for the success of these varieties since they need a great deal of water and have to be protected from floods. The references in the press to the extension of areas under sorghum is an indirect confirmation of the spread of the new varieties, since this cereal constitutes the ideal rotation with them.

Imports of cereals have continued despite the increase in production which seemed, for the first time for a very long period, to be higher than the increase in population. These imports were probably due to the desire to give the communes the maximum reserves in order to allow them to cope with exceptional circumstances, even with a war, as well as to relieve the strain on the railways.

Any judgment on the present state of agriculture must bear in mind the plight of the peasants at the beginning of the present century. From among numerous accounts let me quote that of M. R. S. Nourse, a former professor at Ginghing College in Nanking, taken from her book entitled *The 400 Million:*

In 1911, China was a country which had no middle class; the contrast between the life of the idlers and that of the workers was immense. Most Chinese lived much as if they were beasts of burden . . . Throughout this huge country, there were practically no machines to ease their toil. The rudimentary state of agricultural production forced 80% of the Chinese to work from dawn to dusk. Neither the peasants nor the coolies had any chance of improving their lot. The peasants lived, as they did 2,000 years ago, in mud huts. In the towns, living conditions were much the same . . .

The wretchedness of the peasants is a constantly recurring theme in the history of China, even in its most brilliant ages. The European Jesuits, who settled in China under the Ming, noted that 'the common people often died of hunger and poverty' (Matteo Ricci).

The constant threat of famine had created a veritable art of eking out vegetable resources in case of need. The peasants who had learned through the centuries to distinguish edible species of plants fell back on all kinds of herbs when ordinary sources of food failed. A Chinese scholar in the fifteenth century drew up a detailed inventory of 414 plants grouped in five categories – herbs, trees, cereals, fruits and vegetables, which were eaten in times of famine. Compared to the wretched life of earlier ages, the lot of the peasants under the present regime represents a great step forward.

5. Industrial production and transport

The Chinese is a born craftsman;
one cannot be Chinese without being skilful;
there are no unskilled workers in China.

Henri Michaux

The absence of information, especially statistical information, on the different sectors of industrial production, makes it impossible to assess the position in this area with any degree of accuracy. We have therefore confined ourselves to collecting general data on transport and on the main sectors of industry, while trying to bring out the progress achieved in technology.

The oil industry

Despite the setbacks in the Great Leap Forward and in the subsequent readjustment, there has been a remarkable expansion in the oil sector. Production rose from 1,400,000 tons in 1957 to an estimated total of 10 million tons in 1965, and, according to the American Association of Oil Geologists, to over 16 million tons in 1970. The Chinese Press Agency, without citing figures, announced in September 1970 that drilling teams were striking oil in every region of the country, and that new refineries were being put into operation. This is proof, if any were needed, that, despite the disturbances of the years 1958–60, the difficulties caused by the departure of the foreign experts and the upheavals of the cultural revolution, this industry has been able to make great strides. A centre for oil extraction has been created from scratch at Taching on the sparsely populated plain of northern Manchuria. This success is harped on by the regime, which regards it as a proof of its capacity, 'relying on its own efforts alone', to set up a modern production unit. It also sees it as a refutation of the belief held by the foreigners who formerly controlled China's economy that the soil was poor in oil. In descriptions of China's achievements, Taching is given the star role. In the eyes of the regime, the 'Taching spirit' illustrates the spirit of sacrifice of the pioneers, who have settled in an inhospitable

94

region and created with their own hands their homes and the means to earn their livelihood.

Until Taching went into production, China was short of domestic oil. There were, it is true, the Fushien bituminous shale deposits in the south of the province of Liaoning. The other reserves were located in outlying or not easily accessible regions – at Yumen, more than 2,400 kilometres west of Shanghai, and at Karamai in Sinkiang, not far from Soviet Kazakhstan. The oil was transported to its market some thousands of kilometres away by the new railway line from Urumchi, which was completed in 1961.

Taching, too, is in an outlying region, although its exact location is secret, doubtless for reasons of national security. However, it is common knowledge that the oilfields are in the northwest of the province of Heilungkiang, not far from the Siberian frontier. A refinery has been built on the spot, but most of the oil has to be sent to other refineries. In this sector as in many others, transport constitutes the main problem. The Taching oil, which is near the Transmanchurian railway, is, like the Karamai and Yumen oil, transported by rail, but the number of tank-cars is still small.[1] It is planned to ease the strain wherever possible by recourse to small 20,000-ton tankers for internal and coastal traffic. A Chinese mission visited Europe in the summer of 1970 to place the necessary orders.

In 1969, according to American sources, there were 54 fields being worked, and known reserves amounted to 19,600 million barrels. In 1970, the Peking Government announced the entry into production of a new deposit at Lanchow in Kansu, the centre of a substantial petrochemical industry. It is reported that drilling equipment 'better than the western models' was used on this occasion.

Chinese production is now sufficient for the country's needs, since these are still modest. The number of cars, lorries and tractors is still under 600,000, and almost all current other than hydro-electricity is generated by stations operating on coal. As recently as 1961, China was importing 3 to 4 million tons of oil products. Today, it exports oil – to the People's Republic of Korea – and it is not impossible that in a few years' time hydrocarbons will prove an excellent source of foreign exchange.

There are believed to be considerable reserves, possibly the largest in the world, in the continental plateau under the Chinese Sea. Both

1. This is one of the many points on which we must look to the US observation satellites to provide detailed information.

Japan and Korea lay claims to them, not forgetting Taiwan. If Peking were able to work even a part of these deposits at some future date, it would add substantially to its foreign exchange resources and hence be in a position to expand its foreign trade.

For lack of pipe-lines, natural gas is worked only on a local scale. It is especially plentiful in Szechwan where, as far back as the fifteenth century, if the engravings of the time are a reliable guide, gas was drilled by means of a kind of bamboo derrick. Reserves were estimated by an American source in 1970 at 37 billion cubic metres.

Oil extraction and refining have been carried out since 1960 without any foreign assistance. But, in the period before that date, scores of engineers and technicians were trained in the USSR and Romania. An Oil Institute was set up in Peking in 1953 which turned out 7,000 students in the first eleven years, and China now possesses first-rate technical staff in this field.

Nuclear and arms industry

It was in 1957 that the Chinese Government decided to set up a nuclear industry, and to give priority to the manufacture of atomic bombs. By the treaty of 15 October 1957 it obtained Soviet assistance for the production of nuclear weapons after having created, some six months earlier, an institute of atomic energy.

We do not know the extent of Soviet aid during the two and a half years of its existence, i.e. until the experts were withdrawn in 1960. But the USSR definitely supplied China with a heavy water reactor of from 7,000 to 10,000 kilowatts, which came into commission in September 1958, a 25-million electron volt cyclotron, and some ten accelerators. Almost a thousand Chinese scientists were given special training at the Nuclear Research Institute at Dubna, and the USSR helped in the construction of the isotope separation plant at Lanchow. In a press communiqué of 15 August 1963, which replied to a Soviet Government declaration, the Chinese claimed that the October 1957 treaty was violated on 20 June 1959 by the USSR when it refused to supply China with a prototype of an atomic device, and information on the manufacturing process.

China's uranium atomic bomb experiments in October 1964, which were predicted by the American Secretary of State for Defense as early as 29 September, proved that China's scientists and engineers had succeeded in their undertaking, despite the cessation of Soviet aid. True, the manufacturing processes of such a device are no longer a secret, but the financial, industrial and human resources needed for the actual production seemed to many observers to be beyond China's unaided capacity.

What is remarkable about China's achievement is that it succeeded in completing the isotope separation plant and in producing uranium 238. It was thanks to the enriched uranium from the Lanchow plant that the two plutonium piles at Paotow in Inner Mongolia were, and still are, able to produce such a large number of atomic devices. There are two main reasons for this success: first, the Chinese were able to call on the services of world famous scientists and engineers who returned to the country after 1949, usually on completion of their studies; and secondly, China possesses rich uranium deposits in Sinkiang, together with a hydro-electric station on the Yellow River which supplies the Lanchow isotope separation factory with the necessary power. The nickel and chrome for the manufacture of the tubes for this plant had to be imported.

The Chinese atomic and ballistic programme calls for a wide range of research and development. Thus, in 1959, the Peking Government announced that it was able to manufacture isotope emulsions, counting tubes and neutron spectrographs, heavy particles, and beta and gamma particles.

New techniques have been developed for remote control computers, multi-channel communications, radioelectronics, supersonics and semi-conductors. In 1962, for example, a Chinese source reported that successes had been achieved in the preparation of ultra-pure silicon by chemical and physical means.

The cost of the Chinese atomic programme has been put at about 1 billion dollars a year, or 2% of the 1957 gross national product and 6% of the budget.

Conventional armaments

It looks as if the Chinese leaders have sacrificed conventional armaments to nuclear ones.

Out of the 140 army divisions, only four were armoured in 1965, against fifty in the USSR. There are 3,500,000 men in the regular army, in addition to millions of militiamen trained in people's resistance warfare, but their equipment is primitive. In 1965 the air force had 3,000 aircraft, mostly obsolete models. According to

D

Jane's Fighting Ships, the navy had some 141,000 men in 1970, including 16,000 in the air arm and 28,000 in the marines. Its overall capacity was five times that of Japan's. It was comprised of 33 conventional submarines, 4 destroyers, 8 escort destroyers, 11 other escort ships, 24 submarine pursuit vessels, 394 fast torpedo-boats and rocket-equipped gunboats, 22 coastal defence vessels, 27 mine-sweepers, 70 amphibious and landing ships, 33 auxiliary vessels and 375 service vessels of various kinds.

The Chinese rocket and nuclear aircraft programme

According to information made available to Congress, the American Secret Service believed that, at the end of 1970 or the beginning of 1971, the Chinese would try out their first intercontinental missiles capable of reaching the United States with a 20-kiloton bomb – the equivalent of the bombs that fell on Hiroshima and Nagasaki. As the following table shows, these predictions were not far out.

Chinese Nuclear and Space Experiments

16 October 1964: 20-kiloton atomic bomb, enriched uranium (equivalent of Hiroshima bomb)

14 May 1965: 20- to 70-kiloton atomic bomb, enriched uranium

9 May 1966: 70- to 200-kiloton atomic bomb with thermonuclear elements (lithium 6)

27 October 1966: 20- to 200-kiloton operational enriched uranium bomb on a missile with a range of 600 kilometres

27 December 1966: 300-kiloton thermonuclear bomb

17 June 1967: First hydrogen bomb, 2 to 7 megatons, dropped from an aircraft

3 July 1967: According to Japanese sources, low-powered bomb

27 December 1967: Unsuccessful experiment. No announcement made

28 December 1968: Second hydrogen bomb – possibly operational – 3 megatons

22 September 1969: Underground nuclear explosion

29 September 1969: Third hydrogen bomb, underground explosion

25 April 1970: Orbiting of a 170-kilogram satellite

14 October 1970: Fourth thermonuclear bomb, 3 megatons

3 March 1971: Launching of a second satellite

7 January 1972: Explosion of a nuclear device

18 March 1972: Nuclear device of 20–200 kilotons

The launching base located by the US observation satellites for the first time in 1966 is doubtless in Tibet, and appears to have been completed in 1970 after having been rebuilt in 1969. The Americans believe that by 1975 the Chinese will have from 10 to 25 liquid fuel intercontinental missiles and that, from 1975 on, they will be able to launch solid fuel rockets. China will soon begin to install missiles in the northern parts of the country with a range of 1,600 kilometres. The Americans believe that, by 1975, China will possess 80 to 100 intermediate range missiles of the same type as the one launched with a 10-kiloton nuclear warhead in October 1966.

In addition, China will soon have in operation a bomber with a range of 6,000 kilometres. It is a copy of the Tupolev 16 and is a two-engined jet. It is believed that China is turning out this model at a rate of four to five a month. It can carry several atomic bombs and missiles. According to the London Institute of Strategic Studies, China is in possession of 150 20-kiloton bombs.

The steel industry

Steel production which, prior to 1949, was less than 1 million tons, mostly produced in Manchuria, has benefited from the priority given to heavy industry during the first two Plans, and reached its peak in 1959. Official estimates put production at 18,400,000 tons for that year, but later scaled it down to 15 million tons. Even this lower figure is almost certainly an overestimate, since it includes the inferior steel produced by the rural blast furnaces which had to be used as scrap. Production still fails to meet the nation's needs, and iron and steel products form a high proportion of imports.

The weak points are rolled products and special steels. The quarrel with the Soviet Union broke out when the Russians, whose assistance had made it possible to install equipment in the main steel centres to the stage before rolling, were busy delivering and installing the rolling mills. Deliveries were interrupted, and the Chinese, left to their own devices, had to install 'unaided' the regulating and measuring apparatus. In 1966, therefore, rolling capacity was less than steel capacity. When the cultural revolution started, negotiations had been in progress for over a year with a group of European constructors, led by the Federal German company, Demag, for the purchase of rolling equipment. The talks were broken off at that point. It would be interesting to know whether they are going to be resumed. If they are not, it may be assumed that the Chinese engineers have succeeded in constructing this equipment themselves.

In any case, in 1966, there does not seem to have been a hot continuous broad strip rolling mill, and Japanese experts regarded China as being on an average ten years behind Japan in steel technology at that time.

The production of special steels is constantly being extended to cover a wider range, but it is often only at the experimental stage. Production does not meet national demand. In 1965, China was still unable to produce stainless steel, high temperature steel or high quality alloys.

The showpiece of the Chinese steel industry is the Anshan complex, which has been visited by large numbers of foreigners. By a process of cross-checking, we can form an estimate of its production in 1965 when seven out of ten of its blast furnaces were in production. At that time, it was producing 3,500,000 tons of cast iron, and its steelworks had an output of 3 million tons. Blast furnace number 9 is one of the most efficient in the world. The construction details are first-class, and maintenance is exemplary. It has a volume of 964 square metres and it produces 1,800 tons a day. Its 1250° hot air installation is faultless. The Anshan engineers manufactured the bricks for the vault of magnesium aluminium which can take 1,000 foundings of eleven hours each. Blast furnace number 10, built during the Great Leap Forward, has a volume of 1,513 square metres and an output of 2,400 tons a day, or a ratio of 1·59 tons per square metre.

The main iron mine at Anshan, which produces 2,500,000 tons a year, is efficiently run on the most modern lines.

The Institute for Steel Research of the Province of Liaoning is located in Anshan. It has a laboratory with a staff of a thousand, and its field of work ranges from research on behalf of the Ministry of Industry to any studies required by the iron and steel complex.

China has therefore reached world level in the production of cast iron, but seems to be five years behind, according to Japanese experts, in steel production. However, as early as 1965, the engineers of Anshan and Shichichang succeeded in producing LD oxygen converters without having to buy the foreign patent.

Since the Great Leap Forward, the press has not reported the opening of any new blast furnaces, which suggests that production has edged its way forward only slowly. In 1970, it was announced that a fourth blast furnace, with a volume of 2,516 cubic metres and a capacity of 4,500 tons per day, had been completed at Wuhan, that the Sian steelworks had been equipped with their first oxygen converter, and that some of the small steelworks, which had been closed after the Great Leap Forward, had been reopened.

The electronics industry

Starting from scratch, the Chinese have rapidly succeeded in creating an electronics industry which can satisfy most of the industrial and research needs. Its products cover almost the whole range of appliances and are of high standard, occasionally even comparable to European equivalents, and in any case sufficiently good for the purposes which they have to serve. In this sector of industry, as in all others where technology is constantly evolving, the Chinese have achieved these results by modelling their equipment on imported designs, and modifying and improving the originals wherever possible.

The main centre for the manufacture of electronic apparatus is Shanghai, the Chinese industrial capital. The factories there include one which was completely rebuilt during the Great Leap Forward, and which employs over 2,000 people. Its range of production includes some hundred varieties of apparatus, such as microscopes (including electronic models), spectrographs, polarimeters, collimating lenses, profile projectors, mechanical regulated interferometers, comparators for metrology, and topographical equipment. This factory was built up in only a few years, with mostly Chinese machines and a very youthful labour force. In its equipment and production, it can stand comparison with a European factory. This means that the Chinese are capable, without any foreign help, of building, equipping and running efficiently a modern factory in a sector which calls for highly skilled manpower.

An achievement of this magnitude, in a line of production which was still unknown in China ten years ago, indicates the high level of Chinese ability in the most modern industrial sectors.

Nor is this by any means an isolated instance. Shanghai has other electronic instrument factories. Thus, since 1958, the Hua-Tung factory (in east China) which employs 300 people has been manufacturing extensometric apparatus and strain gauges up to European standards. The same level is attained by another factory, which turns out polarographs, chromatographs, colorimeters and spectrophotometers, all of good quality and manufactured with

101

scrupulous care by young and apparently unspecialised workers.

Visits to factories to which foreigners had access before the cultural revolution revealed the existence of a much more highly developed Chinese industry than expected. According to Japanese experts, however, the electronics industry still has a long way to go in precision and transistorisation instruments. And the capacity for semi-conductors is still inadequate.

China can produce by itself a large number of the electronic appliances needed by its industries, laboratories and universities. Even now, it can dispense with importing appliances in current use. There is no technical obstacle to this industry's expansion, and there is no difficulty about manpower. The rate at which it expands will depend on the financial resources which the Chinese State is willing and able to employ to achieve its economic objectives.

With the cultural revolution over, the Chinese authorities appear to have paid special attention to the electronics industry. The press makes much of the results achieved in the factories in this sector, the number of which is reported to have doubled since the beginning of 1970. The Shanghai industry alone devised 500 innovations and manufactured 300 new products in the course of 1969. Two national conferences on electronics were held in 1970, one in Shantung in March and the other in Peking in May. It may be assumed that the Chinese authorities, in expanding the electronics industry, are seeking to speed up the modernisation of all the other sectors of industry, from metallurgy and oil to machines and means of transport, not forgetting those industries which are working for national defence.

The electronics industry also produces for the Chinese consumer market. During the autumn fair at Canton in 1970, the town's shops were seen to display wireless sets and transistors for the modest price of 20 yuan.

Engineering industries

China has made great progress in the engineering industries since 1958, when these were in their infancy, and in some instances it has achieved a fairly advanced level.

According to Japanese experts, the machine tools industry is the most advanced in the whole engineering industry. In 1965, its production was comparable to the best in the world as regards the lathes manufactured at Shengyang, the rectifying machines, bolts and gears produced at Shanghai and the milling machines at Kunming.

The Chinese excellence in precision engineering is demonstrated, to take an example, by the clockwork factory in Shanghai which was set up as recently as 1958 and which is the first of its kind in the country. Similarly, Japanese experts were impressed by the quality of centrifugal pumps produced in 1965 in the Shanghai factory at the rate of 2,000 a month. These had a diameter of 1,600 millimeters, and their design reflected a familiarity with the latest developments in the theory of hydraulics. The high precision and large capacity pumps were not of such outstanding quality.

In other fields, the technical level in 1965 was very uneven, varying with the category of machines and the order of priority assigned them in the national plan. A great effort had been made to expedite progress in Diesel technique, but China was then far from catching up with Japan in this field. A prototype of an electric locomotive has been designed, but it is not known whether this has been put into large-scale production.

In the electrical industry, according to Japanese experts, China is fairly advanced in power transmission by high voltage grid. Information in this field is scrappy, however. One of the few details revealed in the Chinese press is the construction of 100,000-kilowatt electric turbines in 1968.

The chemical industry

In 1949, the chemical industry was insignificant, but thereafter it developed rapidly, especially after the Great Leap Forward. From 1953 to 1957, priority was given to the basic chemical products – sulphuric acid, ammonium sulphate, caustic soda, chlorine and inorganic salts. From 1958 to 1964, new industries were created or substantially expanded – rubber, fertilisers, pharmaceutical products, plastics and synthetic fibres, for example.

In addition to the ten central research institutes, a network of local institutes has been created all over the country. Progress in the chemical sector may be illustrated by the growing variety of the products manufactured. As early as 1964, the pharmaceutical industry was producing over half a dozen types of antibiotics, including penicillin, streptomycin and tetracyclin. In 1965, the national output of plastics was 28,000 tons – one of the few figures to have been released by the Chinese press since 1960.

In 1965, Japanese experts were of the opinion that the technical level of the Chinese chemical industry was as high as that of their own country in 1950. But China has made great strides forward since then. Most of the plant ordered by China from abroad from 1963 to 1966 consisted of chemical factories using the most modern techniques and producing fertilisers, synthetic fabrics, methanol-octonol and petrochemicals. Chinese engineers are now able to construct such factories by themselves.

Textiles

China is the world's greatest producer of cotton yarn and fabrics – 8·5 billion square metres in 1970 according to Chou En-lai, or just over 10 metres per person.

China is also probably the world's greatest exporter if, as may be assumed, exports are over 10% of production.

Transport

In this densely populated country, draught animals are rare (except in the north), probably because there is nothing to feed them on, and almost all local transport is carried out by man, unaided by any mechanical device. The number of men and women engaged in the daily task of carrying or transporting goods is estimated at several million, both within the cities, between the cities, between the towns and villages, and within the village communities. The new regime has effected hardly any improvement in this field. The 300,000 to 400,000-odd lorries which China possesses can satisfy only the needs of the main factories for their short-distance transport, and those of a very small number of privileged people's communes. In the large towns, such as Peking or Shanghai, in particular, bicycles with trailers are used to move loads which are often quite substantial. But everywhere else, one is struck by the poignant sight of masses of men and women carrying or hauling heavy burdens through the streets as in bygone ages. It will be a long time before these toiling millions will find release. Motorisation has no priority, especially since the labour released by the introduction of mechanical transport would be hard to employ in any other way.

Only a small part of what is produced is transported over long distances in this vast country, which has for so long been partitioned into almost autarkic regions. But this part is of cardinal importance for the country's economic development, for it consists of the raw materials indispensable for industry. It is estimated that coal accounts for 40% of the railway freight traffic, the balance being made up of other heavy raw materials such as cement, oil and cast iron, and bulky commodities such as cereals, cotton and timber which are scarce in many regions and have to come from the out-lying provinces.

Transport by river, especially by the Yangtse Kiang, provides valuable relief, but the navigable network serves only part of the country. The road network, most of it unmetalled, cannot in its present condition take a large volume of traffic, and in any case it is not called upon to do so, since there are not enough lorries. Since 1949, the Chinese have concentrated on the construction of strategic roads in the frontier regions, especially in Tibet. Over 100,000 kilo-metres of roads are reported to have been constructed. It is not known what proportion is metalled.

The main volume of long-distance traffic will therefore continue to be moved by rail for a long time to come. All China's govern-ments have tried to ease this constraint on development, and, well before the 1911 revolution, concessions were granted to companies, mostly foreign ones, for the construction of railways. As early as 1907, however, a company whose capital and personnel were Chinese built a railway without any foreign technical or financial assistance. This project prompted a French journalist to write:

[The Chinese engineers] made a point of showing the Whites that they were able to do a job of this kind by themselves. And they succeeded. Nevertheless, at a certain place, in order to cross a pass, they built too steep a slope, and at that point the locomotives could pull only a small number of waggons. The Europeans, obsessed with their superiority, taunted them with this mistake.

For my part, while I was borne along by the train, I reflected that, only a few years back, the constructors, the administrators, the employees, the telegraphists and indeed the whole staff whether high or low of the railway were, mentally and socially speaking, at the same stage as European peoples some thousands of years back, and I was much more struck by the rapidity of the progress accomplished than by the flaws in the railway itself.[1]

1. F. Arjenel, *A travers la révolution chinoise*, Paris, 1914.

This is a shrewd observation which we would do well to bear in mind in judging present-day China.

Sun Yat-sen had worked out a plan for the extension of the railway network; the Kuomingtang carried out part of this scheme and left China a network of 20,000 kilometres, most of it single-track.

In the course of the First Five Year Plan, the Communist regime allocated to transport a higher proportion of its total investments than the other socialist countries – 15% – of which two-thirds went to the railways. New lines were built and a number of single-track lines were converted to double-track lines, but, from 1960, there was a marked slackening in the pace of construction. In 1966, the length of the network was estimated at 36,500 kilometres, of which only 15% was double-track. If it is remembered that the Japanese network is as large, while serving a much smaller territory, and that the American network is ten times longer, we will realise the burden on the Chinese railways and the priority which its extension deserves. In twenty years, the new regime has put into service a kilometrage which is only just less than the total for the preceding eighty years. Mountain lines, involving the construction of numerous bridges and tunnels, are being built or are planned in the south and southwest, which were up till now the most poorly served. During the cultural revolution, the bridge over the Yangtse at Nanking was inaugurated. This is the second bridge to span the river, the first one being at Wuhan, and the construction raised extremely complex technical problems. In fact, the cultural revolution seems to have given fresh impetus to railway building. Five thousand kilometres were added, bringing the total length to 43,000 (in 1971). However, the whole transport network will have to be even more rapidly expanded in the next ten years if the economy is to grow at the rate of 7 to 8% a year.

China is now endeavouring to manufacture its own railway engines. It is constructing 1,200-h.p. Diesel locomotives, and is planning to dieselise its network, and even to electrify part of it. A prototype of an electric locomotive, developed in 1965, is planned to go into production. According to the New China Press Agency, a first gas turbine locomotive was developed in February 1970. The Chinese-manufactured equipment is of excellent quality and workmanship. Most of the locomotives are based on foreign models. But the Chinese engineers are not content with copying. They engage in research and in the elaboration of original equipment in which they show great inventiveness. They plan to speed up the trains, which are still very slow – the average on the Canton–Peking lines is 50 kilometres an hour – and to automate the marshalling yards. It is with this latter end in view that, in 1965, the Chinese railways purchased abroad a computer for the railway centre of Tsinan, the capital of Shantung. Two orders, one for forty 5,400-kilowatt electric locomotives of the latest model, and the other for fifty 6,000-kilowatt locomotives were placed in April 1970 with a French company, which had already supplied twenty-five locomotives to China in 1958. Another order was placed with a German company, shortly afterwards, for thirty Diesel locomotives.

The Chinese railways have first-class teams of engineers who are fully able to carry out the modernisation of the network. The Railway High School at Peking trains 3,000 pupils, employing as many as 600 teachers and assistants.

The internal air connections cover the whole of the territory, but they are still very sparse, and are available only to the privileged few. China is still entirely dependent on foreign suppliers for its civil aviation equipment, which is of Soviet or British origin. It partially replenished its stock in 1968 by purchases from the Soviet Union, and subsequently in 1970 by buying secondhand Tridents from the Pakistan Air Lines, and six new Tridents in August 1971 from Great Britain.

The only Chinese airlines which fly beyond the country's frontiers are those to Ulan-Bator, Pyong-Yang, Rangoon and Hanoi. The Chinese authorities are anxious, for reasons of prestige, to start flights to Europe, but have no hope of doing so until they can acquire long-distance aircraft. They have accordingly announced their interest in the supersonic Concorde aeroplane, and in August 1971 they invited a mission of the French and British companies manufacturing the aircraft to visit Peking.

The equipment of maritime ports and the merchant navy

Harbour installations are a matter which China cannot keep secret. The foreign crews who land in Chinese ports have noted their inadequacy, which results in very slow turn round.

The merchant navy is still unable to cope with the country's foreign trade. The dockyards can launch only four to five units a year of from 10,000 to 15,000 tons each, or 20,000 tons since the cultural revolution. China purchases from abroad new or second-hand merchant vessels; in 1966 it bought a 20,000-ton liner. It is still obliged to charter 2 million tons of foreign shipping every year.

China is endeavouring to improve its communications, both inside the country and with foreign countries. The restrictions on the import of machines and equipment as a result of the cultural revolution did not affect the transport sector. The recent purchases of locomotives and lorries, and the despatch to Europe in 1970 of missions for the purchase of ships and aircraft, attest the priority attached to communications, if only for strategic reasons.

Main Chinese Production figures
(in millions of tons, unless otherwise indicated)

	Best year before 1949	1952	1957	1962 target in Second Plan (1958–62) (1st version)	1962 target of Second Plan 1958–62 revised in 1969 (Great Leap Forward)	1958 (estimated results)	1958 (official results)[a]	1965 (estimates)	1970 (estimates or official figures)	1971
Cereals[1]	138	154·500	185	250	525	250	270	195	240[3]	246
Cotton		1·300	1·650	2·400	5		2·410	1·7	2·2	
Sugar		0·500	0·864				1·130	1·5	1·7	
Electricity (billions of kilowatts)	5·960	7·260	19·240	44			41·500	50–68	60–100	+8%
Coal	61·880	66·490	130	190–230	380	270	347	225	250–280	
Steel	0·923	1·349	5·350	10·5–12	18	8	13·400	12	18[3]	21
Oil	0·321	0·436	1·460	5·600		2·2	3·700	10	20	25·4
Chemical fertiliser (nitrogen only up to 1957)		0·181	0·800	3·100			1·333	6–8	14[3]	16·8
Cement		2·900	6·860					10	12	+16·5%
Paper		0·600	1·221					1·8	2·5	
Cotton fabrics (billions of metres)		4·200	5					6	8·5[3]	

1. Including potatoes, counted at quarter of their weight.
2. Greatly overestimated in the opinion of the Chinese authorities.
3. Figure mentioned by the Prime Minister in 1971 in a conversation with Edgar Snow.
4. Absolute values in the case of products for which an official figure was published for 1971. In all other cases, since the 1970 figures are only estimates, we have had to make do with the percentage increases for 1971 over 1970.

6. Technical and scientific progress

*We Chinese have played a glorious part in the
development of rockets. At the beginning of
the eleventh century of the Christian era.
Tan Fu and K'I Pu invented them. In the
presence of the emperor, they launched one
into the heavens, using powder as a propellent.
This was the first step on the way to an
artificial earth satellite. The discovery
spread to Europe. Nine centuries later,
a Russian teacher began to interest himself in
the problems of interplanetary space flight ...*

Jen Min Jih Pao (*People's Daily*)

Hardly a day passes without the Chinese press vaunting the newest
successes of the country's scientists, engineers, workers and peasants
in science and technology, industry and agriculture. Newspapers,
reviews and press bulletins headline these feats as proof that China is
capable of attaining the 'most advanced international level'. These
achievements are attributed to the doctrine of economic and
technical independence, and, since 1966, to the cultural revolution.

China today has scientists and engineers as gifted as those of the
main industrial countries and capable of keeping up with them. The
proof lies in their success in developing an atomic device only four
years after the 'defection' of the Soviet experts, and well before the
date forecast by most of the world's experts. In the 1966 experiment
a bomb with thermonuclear elements was tested, and then, in 1970,
an artificial satellite was launched. It took China just over two and a
half years to advance from the atomic bomb to the hydrogen bomb,
whereas it took the USSR three years eleven months, Great
Britain four years eight months, the United States seven years four
months, and France over ten years.

Although it has been given less publicity, the production of
synthetic insulin in 1965, after seven years of research, is also
convincing evidence of the progress of Chinese science. These
developments indicate how China is renewing contact with a
tradition which, up to the fifteenth century, had placed it in the van

110

of technological progress. China, after all, was responsible for such vital inventions as printing, rockets, firearms, the magnetic compass, the spur, the wheel-barrow, deep drilling and the suspension bridge.

Those foreigners – journalists, businessmen, engineers and scientists – who came to China in numbers between 1963 and 1966, were usually impressed by the quality of their opposite numbers. While those who have worked side by side with the Chinese on the shop floor, are forever praising their ability and integrity. They consider that, in comparison with the engineers and workers of other socialist countries, the Chinese come off best. The permanent exhibitions of Chinese industrial equipment at Canton, Shanghai, and other large cities, exhibit machines of a technical level and a range which are beyond most visitors' expectations. The research institutes and laboratories, such as those for physics, pedology, geology, chemistry, electricity and hydraulics, and also the Scientific Academy for Railways, have a large number of researchers, whose equipment is for the most part of good quality. The laboratories of the more important institutes are able to purchase the most advanced apparatus in the world from overseas firms. But much of the equipment is made in China, and many of the institutes have workshops where they can manufacture or repair it. The libraries are well stocked, and subscribe to the latest reviews from all countries. The experiments carried out in the laboratories are of an advanced level, though they are not yet very original.

Most foreign visitors naturally come with preconceived ideas, and are all surprised to find a country by no means backward in science and technology. They have heard so much about the vast toiling masses that they think that China's development is based mainly on large-scale human investment, and are unaware that China already has a considerable number of engineers capable of mastering modern techniques. They admire the technical progress of a country which in 1949 was indebted mainly to foreign initiative for whatever industry it had, and which, out of a population of over 500 million inhabitants, had only 100,000 university level students, 20,000 graduates and 5,000 engineers.

Before taking stock of scientific research and technological innovation in China in 1970, we would do well to take a quick look at the achievements of a civilisation which, although not the oldest one, has lasted the longest.

China's contribution to science and technology

The history of science and technology in China has recently been analysed in Joseph Needham's seven-volume study, *Science and Civilisation in China*.[1] This book shows that the Chinese have made inventions from which they have profited in numerous sectors of production. If, before the publication of this work, there was a tendency to underestimate China's contribution to technology, that is because the country never went through the capitalist stage, and its discoveries were not always applied to industry. It was difficult for foreigners to understand how the Chinese could make important discoveries without these leading to an industrial and social revolution on European lines. The fact is that the Chinese merchant class in the Sung epoch (960–1276) was as prosperous as its counterpart in the Renaissance, but did not invest its capital in industry. This in turn was probably due to the country's system of government. Administration was in the hands of a corps of civil servants who were recruited by competition and who controlled economic activities, and indeed ran them directly when they were of national importance, e.g. the steel industry or the salt works. This corps took umbrage at the creation of private industry, and placed every possible obstacle in the merchants' way. Moreover, the merchants themselves were regarded as socially inferior. They showed no desire to invest in industry and preferred to rise into the nobility by purchasing land, since that was the only form of wealth which conferred social standing in Imperial China.

During the first fourteen centuries of our era, China transmitted a large number of discoveries and inventions to Europe, which was in most cases unaware of their source. The horse's harness, paper, gunpowder, the conversion of rotatory movement into rectilinear movement, the segmented bridge arch, the stern post rudder, all these are Chinese inventions. Anti-smallpox vaccination was known in China as early as the eleventh century. The seismograph, invented by the Chinese in the second century, was long unknown in Europe. The suspension bridge resting on iron chains was devised in China a thousand years before it was known in Europe (in the sixteenth century). The smelting and oxygenation of steel were transmitted to Europe only late in the day.

Firearms were one of China's great inventions, dating back to the

1. Cambridge University Press.

Middle Ages, and yet we are constantly being assured in Europe that the Chinese invented gunpowder only in order to make fireworks, and that the cannon is a European invention which was used at Crécy for the first time in 1346! Yet as far back as the ninth century, in the Tang epoch, a Taoist book mentions a mixture of charcoal, saltpetre (potassium nitrate) and sulphur. In 919, gunpowder was used to ignite a flamethrower. In the year 1000, powder was used to make bombs and grenades (the formula is in a book dated 1044) whereas in Europe it was not till 1285, indeed till 1327, that gunpowder made its appearance. At the beginning of the eleventh century, the Chinese invented the rocket in the form of a bamboo tube filled with a nitrate compound and attached to an arrow.

Scientific research

It was natural for research to be regarded by the Chinese leaders as one of the decisive instruments in economic development, and to be given an important place in the five-year plans. Even in the First Plan, eleven fields had been chosen by the Scientific Academy as deserving priority. They included the peaceful use of atomic energy, iron and steel technology, antibiotics and polymers. The Second Plan (1958–62) concentrated on atomic energy, electronics, automation and remote control. The importance attached by the new regime to research was brought out by the preparation, with Soviet assistance, of a Twelve Year Plan (1956–67) for scientific development. The fields given priority in this Plan were the peaceful uses of atomic energy, jet propulsion, the new electronic techniques, industrial automation, oil and ore prospecting, metallurgy, fuel, heavy equipment, the development of the Yellow River and the Yangtse Kiang, the modernisation of agriculture by means of mechanisation, electrification and chemical fertilisers, and lastly medical research and basic research in the natural sciences.

As in other countries, research work is distributed among national institutions. These are coordinated by the National Commission for Science and Technology, which was created in 1958 and comes directly under the Government. It is headed by Marshal Nieh Jungchen, who studied in France after the First World War. This Commission comprises, among other things, the General State Agency, the Bureau of International Cooperation, the Bureau of Standardisation, and the Bureau in charge of Manufacturing

Industries and Provincial Delegations. Its task is to plan, research, and supervise the execution of the plans.

The main research institution is the Scientific Academy (Academia Sinica) which, up to the cultural revolution, was presided over by a man of letters, Mr Kuomojo. It is divided into five sections, and comprises over 100 research institutes, whose work is coordinated by the provincial delegations of the National Commission for Science and Technology. The Scientific Academy, whose main field is basic research, directs this work with a view to achieving the economic objectives in the plans, and itself follows the directives of the National Commission for Science and Technology. The research institutes, generally headed by a specialist, have as their deputy director or secretary a member of the Communist Party.

Only three fields do not come under the Scientific Academy – medicine, agriculture and armaments, which are subordinated respectively to the Academies of Medical Science, Agricultural Science and Military Science. The first two of these comprise 203 research institutes.

The universities and the other higher educational institutes are equipped with laboratories, but their resources seem to be very slender, since China's skilled manpower is limited, and priority is given to those who do full-time research.

Industry plays a leading role in research, if only because it is regarded by the regime as the main beneficiary. In 1963, there were 354 applied research institutes which came under various ministries, and particularly the Ministries of Machine Construction, which are eight in number.

Industry has control over the coordination of research between the factories and the institutes affiliated to teaching establishments and the Scientific Academy. Numerous research contracts are arranged between industrial enterprises and educational establishments. Cooperation is often carried to the point at which the engineers and researchers form working groups which alternate between the factory and the institution. This system is known as 'mutual loan of staff'.

It is difficult in any country to draw up a balance sheet of the numbers engaged in research, since the personnel are so dispersed. In the case of China we can only guess. However, estimates have been made, for example by Mr Leo A. Orleans in the collection of studies on China published in Washington in 1967 by the Joint Economic Committee.

If we exclude research in medicine and agriculture, it can be estimated that China which, according to *Ten Great Years*, had 32,500 researchers in 1958, had 28,000 scientists and 25,000 engineers in 1965 in research, of whom 3,500 were in the Scientific Academy, 4,500 in university level teaching establishments and 45,000 in the factories and institutes coming under the ministries of industry. To these must be added at least 160,000 Leaving School Certificate students and 200,000 employees and workers. The total would therefore be between 375,000 and 475,000 people engaged in research other than in medicine or agriculture.

As to the cost, Mr Orleans based his calculations on the salaries and wages paid to this staff, and then applied the normal proportion (which in most countries is 40% of this expenditure) to the total cost. He arrived at a figure of 540 million yuan for 1965. On this basis, the expenditure on research in China in 1965 was 1,350 million yuan (or 550 million dollars at the official rate at that time, which is a gross underestimate, of 2·45 yuan to the dollar), 1·1 per cent of the gross national product, which Mr Orleans puts at 120 billion yuan (or 50 billion dollars) for that year. This percentage would have to be scaled down if, as many believe, the figure for the gross national product is really higher. By way of comparison, in 1960 France spent 900 million dollars, and Great Britain over 1,500 million dollars on research and development. These figures will give the reader some idea of the gap between China and the industrialised countries of Europe, not to speak of the USSR and the United States.

Although these estimates are based on somewhat uncertain assumptions, they seem reliable. It should be added that, however poor China may be and however low its *per capita* income, it is able, thanks to its dense population, to raise sufficient resources to carry out research on a scale comparable with that of much richer but less populous states. By concentrating on certain key sectors, such as nuclear and space armaments, it can vie with a power like Great Britain. This is the secret of its success in atomic and space weaponry.

The level of the top researchers is very high. They were all trained abroad: in Japan until Manchuria was annexed by the Japanese, in the United States, Great Britain, France and Germany. Indeed, for some time to come, most of the leading research workers in China will be men who have had their training in the West, since the leading positions are all held by experts with at least ten years' experience.

115

All foreign visitors have been struck by the dearth of high level personnel and by the crowds of bright young researchers. These young men will no doubt take over in the long run, but there has been a break between the generation trained in the West or in the USSR, and the one trained after 1960 in China itself.

The former generation lost all those who did not rally to the new regime after 1949, and decided to stay on in the West. They have been estimated at two-thirds, or about 10,000. They include 4,000 scientists and engineers who remained in the United States, and in many cases now hold high positions. Some of them, it is true, returned to China between 1950 and 1957. The Government of Peking spared no effort in luring back as many as they could of those who had left the country many years before, and whose bourgeois origin tended to alienate them from Communism. The witch hunt in the United States after 1950 greatly aided these efforts, at least until the end of the Hundred Flowers campaign in 1957.

The most famous of the scientists who returned to China from the United States is Ch'ien Hsüeh-shen, born in 1909. He was a graduate of the Massachusetts Institute of Technology and Doctor of Aeronautic Technique at the Californian Institute of Technology in 1939. He has been head of the Chinese rocket programme since 1955, when he succeeded in leaving the United States after a first abortive effort. An American scientist, who knew Ch'ien Hsüeh-shen when he was at the Californian Institute of Technology, regards him as an altogether exceptional personality. He gave the French journalist, Jean Denis, the following pen picture (*Figaro* of 27 July 1970): 'He is an extraordinary man. He astonished both colleagues and students by his capacity for assimilating knowledge. No problem defeated him once he had devoted a couple of weeks to it. Then he out-stripped the expert. When a mind like this is further stimulated by the urge to repay centuries of subjection imposed by the Whites on his people, he can work prodigies.' The American scientist credits the Chinese successes in the development of rockets entirely to Ch'ien's talents. When asked, 'Were you not surprised when the Chinese launched a satellite?' he replied: 'We did not think that China would have the necessary missile so soon. Nevertheless, nothing would surprise me coming from Ch'ien.'

Of the four main Chinese rocket experts, three were trained in the United States, and one in Great Britain. The director of the atomic programme is well known, and has been ever since China tried out

116

its first atomic bomb in 1964. He is Ch'ien San-chiang, Doctor in Physics (1943) of the University of Paris where he was a pupil of Joliot-Curie.

The relations between the researchers and the government authorities fluctuate with the political tide. It is in the nature of a totalitarian regime to subject all citizens to the ideology on which it is based. It is no less normal for the researchers, under any regime whatever, to demand the greatest possible independence in their work. However, it must be said of the Chinese regime that it has not tried to dominate people's thoughts to the same extent as the Stalinists did. It has not elevated a so-called scientific theory to the rank of a State doctrine, as Stalin did with Lysenko's fantasies.

The Chinese leaders are above all concerned to catch up quickly with other industrial countries. They therefore give priority to practical and immediate objectives at the expense of fundamental research, irrespective of the research workers' personal aptitudes and tastes. It is difficult to say who comes off best in this constant tug of war, but the authorities' suspicions of the scientists are, it appears, not entirely unfounded. Doctor Richardson, the director of forestry research in New Zealand, who spent a considerable time in China after 1963, expresses the view in a fully documented work that some of the forestry research seemed to him unsuited to the needs of the economy because those who were engaged on it were inclined to pursue work in China which they had begun during their stay abroad, rather than study the problems which their country's circumstances posed.

Industrial technology

The doctrine of economic and technical independence preached by the Chinese leaders, after the departure of the socialist countries' experts, was inspired by a serious and quite unforeseen situation. The efforts of the whole people who were called on to help overcome the crisis have been successful, and the country's recovery (effected without any foreign assistance) can be termed miraculous. There is no doubt that a challenge of this kind was needed in order to make the Chinese conscious of their ability. Encouraged by their recovery in 1961–64, they now take pride in seeking to master modern techniques by the same methods. They plan to hold in their own hands the keys of their development, and to avoid ever again being at the mercy of foreign experts. They even go as far as to congratulate themselves on the Soviet 'defection' in terms of the dialectic which is dear to them. For this defection, in *their* eyes, was the root cause of their policy of economic independence in which they see the formula for their future power.

No 1 Plastics Factory at Peking (1966)

No 1 plastics factory is one of the ten establishments forming the Peking group of such factories. The group's centre occupies the same site as factory no 1. The Peking plastics factories come under the chemical industries branch of the town council.

Main products:
1. PVC yarn
2. polystyrene yarn

Also soap boxes, cases for transistor sets and alarm clocks, tooth brushes, glasses, combs and car accessories. The raw materials are all of Chinese origin (Peking, Tientsin, Shanghai).

Historical outline. The factory was originally a toothbrush cooperative. It was to meet the market demand that the production of plastic toothbrushes was started after 1956. In that year, production was still at the experimental stage. Since then, considerable difficulties have been encountered, especially during the tests, but the main problems have been solved thanks to Mao's teaching and to the spirit of Yu-Kong, the old man in a famous Chinese fable.

Present equipment in the factory. Part of the equipment was manufactured by the workers themselves (campaign to encourage technical innovations). The rest has been imported, especially from East Germany, Federal Germany, Poland and Japan. Last year, the factory was still buying equipment from abroad.

The work is finished by hand. There is one woman supervisor to each machine. The moulds are manufactured in another Peking factory specialising in that line.

Statement by the factory manager. 'The plastics industry is still very young. It fails to meet demand, especially as regards variety. The quality of the products of the Peking factories is still not as good as those at Tsientsin and Shanghai. A fair number of operations are still carried out by hand. The degree of automation is low. We apply the principle "quantity, quality, rapidity, economy". We try to improve ourselves from outside and also inside. (There is collaboration with the

Tsientsin and Shanghai factories, which send us their engineers and receive our trainees.)'

Planning and designing office. This is what is called the technical section, which prepares plans and designs for the new products. It is this office which receives suggestions for models from the marketing sections.

Consumption → marketing sector → technical sector of factory.

This office has 6 to 7 technicians.

The factory belongs 100% to the State. Its output is sold to a sales company 'in accordance with the State distribution plan'.

Personnel. Total number at present: over 450. This number may vary with the different products which it is decided to manufacture. A month ago, the factory had only 400 workers. The latter move from one factory to another, according to the kind of production required.

Manager: formerly worker in a Peking factory, appointed by the Peking Town Council;

20 engineers and technicians. Oldest engineer – aged 30;

over 300 workers; average age – just over 30;

proportion of women: 46%, including over 10 engineers and technicians (the deputy chief engineer is a woman).

The engineers are trained in different universities and technical institutes; they are then distributed among the factories according to the State's plan; or they 'work their way up' (the factory has three 'technician engineers' who were formerly workers in the toothbrush cooperative).

A fifth of the workers are party members (including members of the Young Communists' League).

Workers study Mao Tse-tung's works as they wish, collectively[1] or individually.

Working hours. Three teams working 8 hours. Forty-eight hour week.

Wages: Monthly wages of best paid engineer 100 yuan
Monthly wages of best paid worker 90 yuan

There are premiums over and above the ordinary wages. These amount to some 5 to 7% of wages.

Almost all workers receive premiums. These are based on the quality of the work etc.

Manufacturing plan. The Planning Committee of the Peking Town Council decides on this as well as on the purchase of machines.

1. Outside working hours.

Part-time work, part-time school. At present a part-time work, part-time study school is being built inside the factory. The course will begin this autumn. This school is directed by the general plastics factory and will take 400 to 500 pupils who will work at the machines four hours a day, and do four hours a day of normal studies. They will start the school at the age of 15. The whole course lasts four years. The courses will stress the general theory of machines and plastics technology. The teachers all belong to the factory. They are either university graduates, or technical institute graduates, or skilled workers.

Foreigners who visited China between 1962 and 1966[1] have often been disconcerted by their hosts' behaviour. They had the impression that the Chinese did not dare to confide in them or to expose their real problems. But this fear of coming out in the open cannot result from any binding instructions from above since, of the tens of thousands of visitors to an exhibition, there are always a few who do give their professional addresses to firms exhibiting their products. But the great majority abstain from doing so out of shyness or lack of confidence. This attitude runs counter to China's real interest, which is to expand and extend contacts with foreigners for, as they themselves admit, they still have much to learn from them.

Foreign missions frequently fail to have a real exchange of views with Chinese engineers. They particularly regret this when, as a result of their visits to factories and their observation of working methods, they are conscious of the improvements that could be effected if they were able to offer advice. The Chinese, it appears, consider it humiliating to ask the visitors their opinion on any point. Many are the visitors who have confined themselves to looking at what they were allowed to see, without seeking to give their Chinese colleagues the benefit of their experience, and without commenting on any defects. Such discretion is sensible. On one occasion an agronomist, well known in the third world for his frank speech and his desire to help developing nations, was lavish with criticism and advice without realising that he was offending his hosts. He was given to understand that his attitude was not appreciated and invited to cut short his visit.

During a visit to a paper factory, members of a European commercial mission noted that a machine manufactured in their country

1. Since that time, foreign missions to exhibitions in China have been few and far between, and the considerations set out in this passage refer to the period preceding the cultural revolution.

was not running properly and that, if that continued, it would certainly deteriorate and finally break down. The mission proposed to send an engineer to China free of charge to put the machine back into working order. The management of the factory declined this offer, possibly fearing that they would be held responsible for the deterioration of the equipment.

We need hardly add that the humility which the Chinese customarily profess is often merely a veneer, and that they are not familiar with the western precept 'moderation in all things', including modesty. Many visitors reply frankly when invited by managers of communes or factories to offer their advice or criticism. But, when they see the expression on their hosts' faces they should realise that polite requests must not be taken literally even in modern China.

With rare exceptions, the Chinese are loath to allow foreign experts to stay in their factories in order to see whether imported machines are running properly. Engineers who have come to China for an exhibition have not even been allowed access to the establishments using the equipment supplied by their companies some years back. The Chinese are probably afraid that the defective operation of a machine will be attributed to their inexperience, and that they will therefore lose face. China is one of the few countries where foreign industrialists are not expected to provide after sales service.[1] Yet many of them would prefer to see their equipment installed and tried out by their own technicians, rather than lose sight of it altogether after it has been delivered. Are the Chinese not carrying their desire for independence too far in thus refusing the cooperation of foreign manufacturers to install machines which even purchasers in the highly industrialised countries do not erect themselves? A Japanese manufacturer, whose Chinese clients had asked for a brochure explaining how to install equipment they had just purchased from him, was obliged to inform them that none existed, and he had a hard time convincing them that he was telling the truth. All his clients, including those from industrialised countries, had until then called in his fitters to install the equipment. This was the first time that a client had not made use of this service. However, in his eagerness to satisfy his clients, the Japanese manufacturer specially prepared a brochure on how to install the machine. It should be added

1. Engineers of western companies who had sold aeronautic equipment to China, and who under the terms of the contract were to stay in Peking during the initial commissioning of the equipment, were never called in for consultation.

that the Chinese conviction that such a brochure can take the place of skilled fitters inevitably leads to some serious disappointments.

This unwillingness to accept advice from foreigners or to allow them entry to their factories, except as visitors, contrasts with the lengthy theoretical and practical cross-questioning to which experts visiting China are subjected. The Peking Government refuses what is usually called 'technical cooperation' for fear of becoming dependent on those willing to provide it and of putting itself in the same class as those countries of the developing world who think that development is possible only under the guidance of foreign experts. The Chinese are too shrewd to deprive themselves of help from abroad. But they are determined to benefit from it as discreetly as possible so as to avoid being regarded as being in receipt of technical assistance.

They have succeeded in profiting from the visits of European and Japanese businessmen, and have used this contact as a means of keeping abreast of the latest technical developments. Most of these foreigners, whatever their special field or the object of their mission, are called upon to deliver what amounts to technical lectures to large audiences. One of the members of a foreign mission observed that the Chinese thus obtained very cheaply a sum total of detailed information which none of the individual members of the mission, all of them highly competent in their own fields, would ever have been able to assemble for his own information. Looked at in this light, the reception of these foreign missions is of greater benefit to the Chinese than many forms of technical cooperation or assistance.

The industrial and technical exhibitions which foreign countries[1] organise in Canton or other cities offer the Chinese, who are quick to seize any opportunity, a chance to put their engineers in direct touch with those of the exhibiting companies. Lectures arranged by the latter are attended by a score or so of Chinese, whose functions – and indeed names – are not disclosed, but who are often leading engineers in their field. In addition to possible purchasers of equipment, the audience includes numerous engineers who are attending with the unavowed intention of obtaining useful tips for use in their own factories. These are really courses on the equipment exhibited, and often last for several hours because of the numerous questions asked by the audience. The commercial effectiveness of these discussions is universally admitted by the industrialists themselves,

1. From 1964 to 1966, Great Britain, Japan, France, Italy, Belgium, Sweden and Denmark organised exhibitions at Peking, Shanghai or Tientsin.

who regard them as the best form of publicity in a market where it is not possible, outside the exhibitions, to make contact with the people who will be using the imported equipment.

Another source of information on foreign sciences and techniques is the systematic exploitation of foreign reviews and publications, especially North American ones.

The Institute of Scientific and Technical Information is in charge of the dissemination, often after translation into Chinese, of all foreign technical and scientific publications or information, including the catalogues of private companies. In 1962, 170 monthly reviews published extracts, translated into Chinese, of scientific documents from all over the world. Considerable resources are used to ensure the widest possible dissemination of the large volume of documentation collected in this way – micro-fiches, orientation courses on patents procured by China from the International Patent Office in Berne, and exhibitions of publications organised around a selected topic, for example, lasers.

All foreigners who have had dealings with representatives of Chinese foreign trading corporations report that these are remarkably well informed, and have read all the literature, especially in the United States, on scientific discoveries and their latest technical applications. One of these officials was seen to possess the house publication of an American company issued as a classified document less than a year earlier.

The Chinese send numerous missions to international congresses and discussions, but, on political grounds, they participate only in those which are held in friendly countries, and exclude delegates from Taiwan.

Negotiations for the conclusion of commercial contracts provide a chance to send Chinese engineers abroad. There, they come into contact with the engineers of companies likely or willing to sell equipment to China, and visit factories which use or manufacture similar equipment.

China is anxious to appear in the eyes of the world, and especially of the Third World, as a country which can manage on its own, and has therefore banned everything in its foreign relations which savours of the technical assistance provided by the industrialised countries to the developing world.

However, scientific and technical circles regard this forced isolation as irksome and harmful to their interests, and it is possible

123

that they may induce the political authorities, despite the cultural revolution's ban on contacts with foreigners, to accept certain forms of scientific and technical cooperation, at least to a limited extent and in such a way as to keep up an appearance that each side is gaining something. In so doing, the Chinese leaders would, as often happens, be adopting a more realistic and less dogmatic line than the one laid down in their propaganda.

Before the cultural revolution, China had begun to cooperate with certain countries. In October 1964, conversations took place at Peking between the Academy of Science and the President of the British Royal Society. There were plans for an exchange of scientists. The Chinese were anxious, as a first step, to send to Great Britain experts in bacteriology, geology – especially for work on radioactive dating – and biophysics. As a second priority, they mentioned high energy physics, molecular biology and heart surgery. In October 1965 an agreement was signed between France and China for cultural and technical cooperation. It provided for the exchange of technical missions, and the organisation of training courses for students and research workers in education and research institutions, but not in industrial firms. This is the only agreement concluded between China and a western European country. It is not known how far it has been implemented. It probably did not get very far, since the cultural revolution broke out soon after the agreement was signed.

The most obvious, and also the cheapest, way of raising the technological level of a country is to copy foreign equipment. The less developed countries always tend to draw on the achievements of the more developed ones, and there is no exception to this rule. In Europe it was the same. Readers may remember the story of the continental industrialist who, at the beginning of the nineteenth century, smuggled out of England, under his greatcoat, the designs of the latest textile machines. The Chinese make no bones about admitting that they copy other nations' models, since for a considerable time even Japan obtained its technical knowledge in this way. Chou En-lai himself urged his compatriots, in a report on economic policy to the National Assembly on 21 and 22 December 1964, to 'absorb everything that was good in other countries' experience and techniques'. 'But', he added, 'the lesson learnt from them must be blended with a creative effort on our part.' The Chinese copy is usually an intelligent one. It takes account of the specific conditions of the country, its topography and the raw material specifications.

A foreign mission observed, when visiting the Wusung refinery near Shanghai, two topping towers side by side – one of them Russian and the other Chinese. The latter was obviously a copy of the former, but with judicious modifications.

However, the Chinese are not always fortunate in their choice of apparatus to be copied. For example, they reproduced, down to the smallest detail, a farming machine constructed by a small Japanese firm without realising that it was badly designed and that its manufacturer had gone bankrupt. By the time they realised their mistake the machine had been put into large-scale production. Another instance of an expensive and unsuccessful copying operation is cited by the Japanese. Chinese engineers reproduced a twenty-year-old model of a car engine, but they equipped it with such heavy accessories that the vehicle could only run at a snail's pace. However, the Chinese do not copy all the equipment imported, and numerous cases could be given of orders for several models of the same machine which have been periodically repeated.

As they are able to manufacture an increasing range of equipment independently, and to apply the procedures and methods already tried out in other countries, the Chinese, when buying machinery abroad, are interested only in the most modern types embodying techniques which their engineers have not yet completely mastered. Nevertheless, quite a few cases could be listed of perfectly standard machinery which the Chinese have been buying abroad regularly for many years.

Even some foreign companies exhibiting in China have to be careful to offer competitive goods. The Chinese are fond of telling the story of an electronic microscope which magnified 120,000 times and was exhibited in Peking in November 1964 by a British firm. The article was not purchased, since Chinese industry was already producing a type which magnified 200,000 times. They proudly add that China constructed its first electronic microscope in 1957, and it magnified 50,000 times. The Japanese were more successful than the British. At a specialised exhibition, they demonstrated a microscope which magnified 250,000 times, and they sold about a dozen of them.

Whatever the capacity of the Chinese engineers and their success in theoretical studies, they often lack that general insight which is not to be found in any textbook and which we call 'know-how'. This cannot be bought with a patent. The knowledge that Chinese engineers have acquired comes from the best sources and is completely assimilated, and yet there is often something bookish and

125

theoretical about it. For example, the Chinese colleagues of some European engineers building a factory in China asked them to use transistors at a time when these had never been used anywhere. They had read in some review, doubtless an American one, an article on the subject, and could not believe that the ideas expressed there could not be applied immediately. Chinese engineers, in short, tend to think that they can solve any technical problem where the detailed solution is presented to them in written form.

It is therefore understandable that the Chinese leaders should endeavour to fill the gaps in a very recently developed industrial tradition, and campaign for a closer association of theory and practice in studies. This desire to train technicians along realistic lines is reflected in the spread of secondary schools, in which the student's time is divided between theoretical exercises and work in the factory, and where they are also obliged to work for several weeks a year in the fields or in the factories. In China, engineers are used to lending a hand in the factory or in the workshops. One of their most brilliant oil engineers was seen by a foreign mission to climb up a derrick when the thermometer was below zero in order personally to carry out some repairs.

Such a policy of learning as one goes inevitably means a certain number of mistakes and delays. The time needed to bring into production the new factories built by the Chinese themselves is considerable, and many of the machines which they try to design and construct without foreign help have to be thrown on the scrap heap. Far from concealing such setbacks, most factory managers admit that they have had to overcome a whole string of difficulties. They even take pleasure in listing them, as if to emphasise the merit attaching to their final victory.

Chinese methods and objectives as regards technological development can be illustrated by the construction in 1965 of a 12,000-ton hydraulic press, details of which captured the headlines in the Chinese papers for months. The *Peking Review* of 15 March 1965, for example, gives an edifying account of this enterprise which (with some justice according to foreign specialists) has filled the Chinese with pride. The *Review* takes us back to what is almost a handicraft, pre-industrial era. It relates with a wealth of detail how, without modern machinery but drawing on foreign publications, the workers and cadres of the factories were able, after years of efforts and experiments, to finish their assignment. No doubt a country with modern production means would have needed only a few months to construct the same machine. The fact remains that, contrary to rumours, it works, and this success has impressed quite a few previously sceptical foreign engineers.

The number of machines which Chinese industry is capable of producing without foreign help is increasing rapidly, as can be confirmed by a visit to the permanent industrial exhibitions in Shanghai or Shenyang. Admittedly, some of the machines exhibited are only prototypes, but their construction was believed to be beyond the Chinese capacity. The machines produced in 1865 included the equipment for a urea factory in Shanghai, a gamma-ray emitter, an artificial heart and lung, a globule counter, a high-pressure nitrogen and hydrogen compressor, an 8,000-h.p. Diesel engine, a 6,000-kilowatt gas turbine – replacing a 1,500-kilowatt one in 1964 – a 100,000-kilowatt turbo-generator, a capillary chromatograph, a high-speed electronic calculator, an analogue computer, a telescope, an electronic bombardment chamber, an infra-red spectrophotometer, a transistorised photoelectric cell switch, an isotope separator and a semi-automatic universal rectifying machine.

China possesses a fair number of industrial plants which are up to European standards. We may mention some of those to which foreigners had access before the cultural revolution:

A lorry factory at Changchun in Kirin Province, which produced 30,000 5-ton lorries in 1964 (or one every six minutes) and most of whose installations are modern.

The No 1 machine-tool factory in Peking, which produces 2,400 milling machines a year and whose workshops, except for the foundry, are well equipped and organised.

The tractor factory at Loyang, which turns out some 50 tractors a day.

The Shanghai Diesel engine factory which is relatively fully automated, Chinese from start to finish, and which manufactures 30- to 250-h.p. Diesel engines. This is a model designed by the Chinese and believed to be one of the largest in the world.

The Sin-An-Kiang hydraulic generator in Chekiang, all of whose components were constructed in Chian, usually on the basis of Soviet designs. These components are of good quality and, a significant point, the turbines are quiet even with a 90% load.

A lesser known and rarely visited factory in Shanghai which manufactures thousands of oscilloscopes and other electronic measuring instruments; the equipment is fairly simple, but the products are of excellent quality.

127

No doubt many of the modern factories were inherited from the Russians. But not all of them were completed when the Soviet experts left, and the Chinese must be given credit for having completed and sometimes improved their machinery and put it into production.

The main defect of the Chinese industrial plants, as it is of Soviet factories, is the poor organisation of labour. The divergence in the rates of production of the different workshops leads to congestion at certain points, and this is the reason for that impression of confusion which the visitor often carries away with him when leaving these establishments.

Coke and Chemical Products Factory at Peking (1966)

The factory is located 15 kilometres southeast of Peking, and produces coke, gas and by-products.

It was built during the Great Leap Forward in only eight months – from March to November 1959 – and was designed entirely by the Chinese. The plans were prepared by the Anshan Steel Institute, which continues to supervise the factory and in a way provides the technical management.

The factory's equipment was entirely manufactured in China. The coking equipment came from Dairen, the conveyors from Peking and the refractory material from Anshan.

Annual production:

1,000,000 tons of coke
  15,000 tons of benzol
  50,000 tons of pitch
  12,000 tons of ammonia
  500,000,000 cubic metres of gas – 300 million for the factory (coking oven and by-products; 200 million cubic metres are distributed in the city of Peking to serve 400,000 people).

This factory supplies all the gas consumed in Peking. The gasometers, with a capacity of 110,000 cubic metres, are said to be nearer the town. Production is stationary, but it will increase by 50% when a third battery of ovens starts to operate at the end of 1966.

Productivity. This is stationary, for production and personnel are stable, but it will increase sharply when the third battery of ovens goes into production, since there will be no great increase in personnel.

Personnel.
Total strength: 2,100, of which 20% are women, the proportion being highest in administration.

Engineers: 20
Technicians: 100
Employees: 200
Workers: just over 1,700, of which 90% are skilled.

Only one or two engineers have come up from the ranks, and there does not seem to be any established policy for promoting workers. Promotion seems to be mainly by seniority. The workers are grouped into eight categories, as in any factories in China.

Wages. The average monthly wage is 61 yuan, and it is calculated for the staff as a whole, without taking any account of the size of each category of wage-earners.

Premiums. About 15% of the total volume of wages. Monthly average per person: 3·60 yuan. Formerly, premiums were awarded in the course of staff 'assemblies' and fixed by general consent for three categories of beneficiary. At present, the whole staff receives a single premium of 3 yuan per person. The remaining 0·60 yuan (on an average) come from a small premium received by a few key workers and employees, every three months, and this is paid not in cash but in kind, for example in clothes, works by Chairman Mao etc. 'Political consciousness' plays a great part in the premium system. For example, in 1965 the 'model workers' refused the premiums which their comrades had suggested should be awarded them.

Origin and quality of staff. When it was set up, the factory had only ten specialised workers from other coke works. Most of the workers were provided by the People's Army, who were demobilised but retained their rank and organisation intact. Visitors are received by one of the managers of the factory, accompanied by an administrator and a technician. He is an ex-officer, demobilised in 1955, and he joined the factory in 1960 after several periods of training in other factories. He is particularly friendly and articulate, and appears to be very competent, but he affects great modesty and keeps on saying that he is not very knowledgeable. He dwells on the serious difficulties encountered at the start owing to lack of skilled personnel, workers and cadres.

The specialised workers trained elsewhere than in the factory come from Shih Ching Shan and Anshan. It takes a year to train a worker, which seems rather long, since there is practically no technology to be

E

picked up, only a certain know-how. The cadres and engineers who joined the factory in 1959 had taken their diplomas as recently as 1954. Most of these cadres (70 to 80%) joined in 1960 on completion of their studies. The administrative cadres come from administration or are former officers. 'We started from scratch, and so we must learn as we go. The training of staff is our major problem. We are still behind the older factories and the quality of our coke is not as good as at Shih Ching Shan.'

Management of the enterprise. As long as the prices of coke and coal were roughly equal, there was a loss which was borne by the State. Now the price of coke has been slightly increased, and there is still a loss. But losses and profits are meaningless, for everything comes from and goes to the State. 'We pay in tax about 20% of the turnover. Taxes don't mean much. We give the State money, and it gives us funds for our investments. For some time (it was not specified for how long), we have not drawn on our own resources for self-financing. Everything goes to the State, which gives us money if we need any.'

Plan. 'There is an annual plan, but it has changed little, since we have been working to full capacity for some years . . . The plan is fixed after discussions on the proposals by the planning body and by the enterprise. When an enterprise does not meet its target, sanctions are taken, but no enterprise has so far failed to do so.'

7. The Cultural Revolution

Carry out the Revolution and Increase Production.
Slogan of the cultural revolution

I am alone with the masses.
Mao to Malraux,
Antimemoirs, 1966

Social and economic aspects

The cultural revolution was directly in the Chinese tradition. Its main object was to accomplish an intellectual and moral reformation. In launching it in 1968, Mao Tse-tung set out to denounce Khrushchev's 'goulash communism' and reaffirm the principles of genuine socialism.

To the political objective of the movement was added an economic one. The former was meant to purge the masses, that is to say, all those outside the party cadres; the latter was designed to fan revolutionary fervour and stimulate production. The participation of the masses was to be the best guarantee of productivity.

There has been a tendency to regard the cultural revolution as ideological in its essence and political in its effects, and accordingly to neglect the social and economic factors which partly explain its gestation and evolution.

The Great Leap Forward did not produce the results anticipated. If structural modifications had not been enough to bring about a radical change in the economy, was this not proof that there was need for an ethical revolution, for man himself to be changed – an idea not unfamiliar to the Chinese? By changing man himself, without sitting back and waiting for this to happen through a transformation of the infrastructure (as is recommended by a mechanistic conception of Marxism), would it not be possible to create a new order of society in which the productive forces would become fully effective? The transformation of moral forces into physical ones is expected to bring about a kind of miracle, for 'as long as there are men, miracles of all sorts can be performed under the leadership of the Chinese Communist party.' This basic

131

confidence in man assumes that, once he is freed from the fetters of the old society, he will be able to enter the golden age, as assumed by Rousseau. This was the origin of the Great Leap Forward, which had not only ethical but also economic objectives. In Mao's view, the Great Leap Forward was the answer to the problem of Chinese poverty.

By a piece of dialectic reasoning characteristic of Chinese thought, Mao proposes to see in his country's poverty a positive factor, for, as he says poetically, 'on a blank page everything is possible; one can write on it whatever is newest and finest'. The realisation of China's poverty is matched by complete confidence in its future:

'The Chinese people has both will-power and ability. In the not too distant future, it will catch up with and overtake the most advanced countries in the world.' This statement of Mao's was taken a stage further by a journalist writing at the height of the cultural revolution, who asserted: 'All the imperialist and revisionist countries will one day be left far behind; about this there can be no doubt at all.'

It has not been sufficiently stressed that, according to the doctrine of the cultural revolution, productive capacity is more strongly stimulated by socialist consciousness than by material incentives. 'While we recognise', wrote Mao Tse-tung, 'that, in the general course of historical development, the material determines the spiritual, and social being determines social consciousness, we recognise, and must recognise, the feedback of the spiritual to the material, and of social consciousness to economic being.' As a Shanghai paper noted in August 1967: 'Of the thousand and one means of developing socialist production, the most important is to drive ahead vigorously with the revolution on the political and ideological planes. If that action is successful, there will be an increase in the production of cereals, cotton, oil, steel, cast iron and coal. If not, it will mean failure.'

According to the makers of the cultural revolution, the productive capacity of the masses will be further stimulated by the greater equality between citizens. They believe it is easier for people to accept austerity when the level of life is the same for all and there are no distinctive external signs of wealth. The ideal society, according to these thinkers, glorifies manual labour and the simple virtues of country life. In this, and in its condemnation of luxury, this ideal echoes Jean-Jacques Rousseau's model society. The author of the *Social Contract*, with whose works many Chinese are familiar, was one of the writers from whom Maoist philosophy grew and continues to draw its inspiration.

This egalitarianism, which may appear out of place in a modern industrial world founded on the division of labour and hence on the diversification of social status, is, according to Mao, in harmony with Chinese reality, that is, with a society too poor to tolerate inequalities, especially since the vast majority of the people have been kept in a state of subjection for centuries.

The desire for an egalitarian society was frustrated by the persistence of class difference. Mao Tse-tung was skilful enough, on seizing power, to try to win over the middle classes, as he reckoned their contribution was vital to the reconstruction of the nation. Even before 1949, young middle-class men and women, exasperated by the Kuomintang's ineptitude, settled in Yenan in order to follow the courses at the anti-Japanese university. Many of them rallied to Mao out of nationalism, since they regarded him as the only man capable of freeing China from its semi-colonial shackles. In the years following the 'liberation' (the use of the term in preference to 'revolution' is significant), the intelligentsia and the liberal and industrial professions were spared, whereas most of the landowners or elements regarded as 'beyond recovery' were liquidated.

The regime owed its victory to an illiterate peasant army, and it needed cadres too badly to dispense with the existing ones, even those that were uncommitted or even hostile. As is well known, even industrialists defined as 'bourgeois national' still held responsible positions in the factories they previously owned. As late as 1965, most of the students were of bourgeois origin, although the proportion of peasants' and workers' sons was rising (28% in 1955; 36% in 1958; 42% in 1962; and 49% in 1965). The number of leading positions in industry and administration still held by the middle class was considerable. All the foreigners who visited China before the cultural revolution were struck by the fact that most of the men they dealt with in official circles were of non-proletarian origin. It was not unusual, in a factory run by a revolutionary veteran, to see him flanked by a technical adviser belonging to the former ruling class. Most of the teachers, scientists, and research workers were drawn from the middle class – the only class whose children had been able to study under the previous regime. This middle-class

133

background was in fact common to all those in responsible positions who were over forty in 1965. The dominating role of the middle class in economic and intellectual life at that time led Mao to fear that the country might be led away from socialism.

The aim of the men behind the cultural revolution was to establish a proletarian and egalitarian society in which the whole of the people would take part in political and economic life in order to raise productivity. It is difficult to say to what extent this ideal has been realised in the social and economic order. But it is certain that the structures have not been modified as drastically as the cultural revolutionaries had wanted. For instance, we have seen how the peasants have retained their family plots. But only the future will tell us whether new management methods, especially in the factories, have been established on a lasting basis and how effective they are.

The effects of the cultural revolution on production

In 1967 the confused political situation in the large towns, and the interference in the work of the production units by factional struggles, created the impression that China was on the verge of an economic crisis every bit as serious as the one that followed the Great Leap Forward; that she was, indeed, about to sink into chaos. The ideological war in the factories threatened to spread to the countryside, and on several occasions paralysed the vitally important flow of supplies to the modern industrial sector and of food to the towns. However, once the cultural revolution was over, it became clear that the damage to the economy was not as serious as had been expected. The industrial system was never completely dislocated. The cultural revolutionaries were careful, when they saw that the struggle might degenerate into a serious clash, to apply the brakes and to launch the slogan: 'Carry out the revolution and expand production.' The ideological struggle was not to be allowed to divert the militants from their obligation to produce.

An example of Cultural History during the Cultural Revolution

At the height of the cultural revolution, a European businessman who was attending the Canton Fair was chatting with a Chinese interpreter while waiting for an appointment. The two were alone.

The businessman complimented the interpreter on his English. As the latter told the visitor that he had started to learn French too, the European made a few remarks about the vocabulary common to both languages. The interpreter than gave a detailed account of the relations between France and England since the time of William the Conqueror, went back even further to the Roman influence on England and, when the businessman mentioned Hadrian's wall, added without any prompting: 'Yes, the wall that was built to keep out the Picts and Scots.'

It will be seen that the programmes of the School for Foreign Trade do not leave out history and that, even at the height of the cultural revolution, a young Chinese was not afraid to air his knowledge on a subject which had nothing to do with current issues.

A good indication of the damage done to the economy may be derived from the only figures available to us – those for foreign trade. The import figures were 4·3 billion dollars in 1966, just below the record of 4·5 billion dollars attained in 1965, and 4·35 in 1959. In 1967 the value fell to 3·8, and to 3·6 in 1968. In 1969, it turned upwards to about 3·9 billion. Exports fell by 15% in 1967, and by 1·6% in 1968. There is a clear parallel between the dip in foreign trade and the impact of the cultural revolution. The year in which that impact was greatest in the cities was 1967. In that year, the fall in exports corroborates the dip in industrial production, which was estimated at between 15 and 20%. For food products, it was the dislocation of transport and the breakdown in administration that explained the fall in exports. From 1968 on, exports of rice and pigs to Hong Kong were resumed.

Imports, too, suffered from the cultural revolution. They fell by over 13% from 1966 to 1967, and in 1968 remained almost stationary. Imports of equipment and machines were the most seriously affected. Does this reflect new and extreme views of the Chinese technical ministries, with regard to the benefits of economic independence and total denial of any foreign contribution? As early as the autumn of 1966, the import corporations broke off their talks with foreign industrialists; and the step was explained in this way: 'We are no longer interested in importing this type of factory. During the cultural revolution, the workers and the technicians concerned discussed the question thoroughly and came to the conclusion that the technique applied in this type of foreign factory may well be advanced in certain respects, but is not necessarily superior to the Chinese technique.' This was the way negotiations

135

with the German Demag group were broken off, although what was at stake was a rolling unit indispensable to the Chinese steel industry if it is to increase its production of sheet iron.

Of the contracts being carried out at the time the cultural revolution began, some were completed satisfactorily, for example a bank-note factory ordered from France in 1966, and the chemical factory at Sseu-Chuan from Great Britain. Admittedly, obstacles were sometimes placed in the way of the work. Foreign engineers and technicians were arrested, and one of them sentenced to prison for espionage. The excitement aroused by the cultural revolution led the most fanatical to suspect all foreigners of evil designs. At Lanchow, the Chinese decided to dispense with the services of the German Lurgi company which was installing a petro-chemical plant, and handed the job over to their own engineers. It was recently rumoured in Germany that China had just ordered spare parts for this factory which should not have been needed for some ten years. It is there-fore supposed that serious errors were made in assembling the unfamiliar equipment.

It remains to be seen whether this refusal to import foreign technology, either in the form of licences or capital goods, will survive the end of the cultural revolution. If this turns out to be so, it will be of great importance for the future. One of the slogans of the cultural revolution denounced infatuation with foreign techniques, and emphasised the need to give priority to Chinese techniques. Unless the Chinese are capable of mastering the latest techniques in all fields without help, as the Soviets did from 1930 on, this technological autarky is likely to cost them dear and slow down their development. In any case, the path they have followed is diametrically opposite to the one chosen by Japan, which continues to base its technological development on the purchase of foreign licences, even though it is increasingly able to work out the tech-niques required.

It will be interesting in the near future to see whether the dis-cussions which were broken off during the cultural revolution will be resumed and whether others will be started. The announcement in 1970 in *China Reconstructs* of the installation at the Shih Ching Shan factory near Peking of a large rolling-mill suggests an answer, for it seems possible that this plant (about which the article in the review gives no details) is intended to replace the one that was to be bought from Germany. It should, however, be noted that three Chinese missions visited Europe in 1970 to study the possibility of purchasing machine-tools, ships and aircraft, and that there appears to be a revival of interest in the purchase of factories on the part of the Chinese foreign trade corporations. An order for six Trident 2E's at a cost of 48 million dollars was placed on 24 August 1971 with Hawker Siddeley, and new Chinese missions, including one on telecommunications, travelled to Europe in 1971. The recent increase in the number of Chinese missions to Japan and Europe makes it probable that purchases of complete factories will shortly be resumed.

The other import items, after having dropped in 1967, increased in 1968, and rose even further in 1969. This was true of fertilisers, which suggests that increased agricultural production, despite the progress already made, is still a basic objective. There has also been an increase in imports of steel products and non-ferrous metals, which are indispensable for the armament industries – nickel, copper and lead.

If checked against other sources, the data on foreign trade enable us to measure the effects of the cultural revolution in the various sectors of the economy. The 1967 cereal harvest is generally agreed to be one of the best ever recorded, perhaps indeed the best in the history of China, and is estimated at from 200 to 230 million tons. Yet 1967 was the year in which the cultural revolution was at its height. However, one must take into account the vital fact that the weather was very favourable in that year, which it was not during the year of the Great Leap Forward. Moreover, the peasants were not diverted from their work by reading Mao's teaching. And if they *did* read him, their study did not encroach on the time they spent in the fields.

If we assume the 1967 harvest to have been 215 million tons, to take a figure midway between the various estimates, the increase over 1957 would be 16%, and hence much the same as the increase in population. It is in fact probable that the population increased on an average by 1·5% a year from 1957 on, for in 1960 and 1961 there was a fall in the birth rate and an increase in the death rate. On this assumption, the *per capita* availability of cereals would be much the same as in 1957, which tallies with the impressions of most foreign observers. It seems that the 1968 cereal harvest was worse than the 1967 one, although Peking announced that 'crops were abundant'. The wall newspapers for their part reported the prime minister as being pessimistic about the supply of fertilisers which, he said, had fallen by 50%.

Industry, as already stated, was far more seriously affected by the cultural revolution than agriculture. Its output fell by 15 to 20% in 1967, and then turned upwards in 1968, except in those regions where the disturbances continued, as in Wuhan where the troops actually used their weapons.

In considering the factors responsible for this fall in output, it is difficult to distinguish between those peculiar to each sector, such as the intensity of the political struggle inside the factories, and the external causes such as the poor flow of supplies of raw materials and semi-finished products caused by the disruption of transport. The railway workers' strikes and the strain caused by the Red Guards' travelling prevented the railways from moving the usual amount of commodities needed by the factories.

Article 12 of the Charter of the cultural revolution, published on 8 August 1966, lays down the following rules:
> Policy as regards scientists, engineers and technicians:
> Scientists, engineers and technicians, if they are patriots, if they do their work well, if they are not hostile to the party and to socialism, and if they do not maintain illegal relations with foreign countries, should be treated as follows. We should for the moment continue to apply to them the policy of 'unity, criticism, unity'. Particular regard should be paid to scientists and technicians who have made useful discoveries. Efforts should be made to assist them gradually to modify their world views and their mode of work.

There were shortages of coal and oil, but it is not known to what extent these were due to lack of transport or breakdowns in production. The coal industry was racked by bitter political struggles in 1967. Two conferences were held in 1968 to deal with these problems, and a campaign was launched to invite the population to economise on coal.

The oil industry was also rent by rival factions. Even at Taching, work is said to have stopped completely, and the workers sent off to stimulate the cultural revolution in the towns. And yet, in 1968, the Peking press announced that, in the oil sector, the Third Five Year Plan (1966–70) had been fulfilled two years ahead of time.

The explanation seems to be that all sectors of industry were hit in 1967, but that there was a recovery about the middle of 1968. For their part, the official information services continued throughout the cultural revolution to headline technical innovations and new investments, as if to demonstrate that economic progress was not being held up.

The cultural revolution certainly involved a loss of production, but it also showed the maturity of Chinese industry. The drop in production is generally agreed to have been relatively slight, given the bitterness of the political struggles. On the whole, Chinese production stood up to the ordeal successfully, especially if one remembers that most of the technical cadres must have been grilled about their ideological orthodoxy and criticised about their ideas; a fair number of them were removed from their posts – at least for a time.

The cultural revolution and the position inside the enterprises

The effects of the cultural revolution on the enterprises are known to us only from the few reports of foreigners allowed to visit industrial plants in the autumn of 1967, once the fight for power inside the factories was, by and large, over.

In a Peking machine tool factory, Joan Robinson was able to talk with the personnel in October 1967. At that time, power was in the hands of the Triple Alliance – the revolutionary cadres, the workers and the militia. The revolutionary committee was responsible for running the plant, and its directives were carried out by three offices – those for policy, administration and production, whose leaders were members of the committee.

In this way the party committee, which had been the leading body in the enterprise before the cultural revolution, was obliged to surrender control to a new body formed in the battle against it. The party committee was accused of anti-democratic methods, i.e. of allotting the real power of decision to the technical cadres and imposing these decisions on the workers without allowing any discussion.

In this factory the struggle for power had been settled without violence. It had taken the form of a debate on management, and victory had gone to those who had won over the majority of the workers to their views. Of the cadres which were criticised, those who finally admitted their errors were allowed to join the revolutionary committee and given a job in the workshop, where they found an opportunity to 'reform their minds by productive work'.

Another example cited in Joan Robinson's book is that of a

confectionery factory in Shanghai. The 'bad' cadres here also were posted to the workshop. The number of cadres was reduced by 42%. The factory is now run by a revolutionary committee of eleven.

The main effect of the cultural revolution has therefore been to replace the party committee by the revolutionary committee. The management is still collective, but the real leaders are no longer the party members. They are those who, at the end of a frequently lengthy battle within the enterprise, have succeeded in imposing the doctrine of the cultural revolution. It is they who represent the will of the masses, and who mean to run the enterprise in accordance with the teachings of Chairman Mao, replacing material incentives by ideological ones, and enabling all the workers to take part in running the factory by explaining to them what is expected of them, by taking account of their suggestions and by giving them scope for their initiative.

The criticism of the party machine by the Maoists, and the humiliations heaped on a number of its members, were widely regarded as reprehensible or ill-advised. The most obvious result was to undermine the party and to deprive it of its authority over the masses. In a country where it is vital for the central government, however flexible its policy, to impose its directives and to ensure that they are applied throughout its territory, the weakening of the party may deprive the State of a major instrument for asserting its authority. This state of affairs, it was argued, might encourage the particularist tendencies and centrifugal movements, which are constant in China's history.

As against this, it should be stressed that the methods used by the party cadres to settle the country's affairs before the cultural revolution were by no means perfect. In all communist countries there is a danger that the cadres will take advantage of their considerable powers to force their views upon the people without letting them express their own opinions or take part in open discussions. Once on this wrong track, the cadres can paralyse institutions and discourage people who were originally well disposed to them.

It is clearly very difficult for a foreigner to fully understand this vital and delicate issue of the party's relations with the population which it is supposed to 'officer'. But it seems certain that there was violent argument on the subject within the party, since one of the Maoists' main aims in the cultural revolution was to incite the masses to rebel against the cadres' misuse of their power.

Incentives

Incentives to increase production were at the heart of crucial debates in the cultural revolution, for the Maoist ideology calls for the suppression of incentives at some point in time. It plans to rely solely on the workers' professional conscience, or rather on their socialist conscience, to increase productivity. In terms of this ideology it is axiomatic that they will respond to such political incentives, since they are no longer working for a master who exploits them, but for society. This type of incentive has been considered inadequate by European socialist countries, which tend to rely decreasingly on 'socialist emulation' to expand the economy as their standard of living rises. Even in Cuba it seems to have been proved that enthusiasm cannot take the place of material incentives. But the Chinese leaders have set out on the opposite track, at the very moment when these other countries are putting more and more emphasis on *material* incentives. To increase production, the Chinese propose to rely exclusively on the devotion and spirit of sacrifice of the workers, to whom they hold out the prospect of transforming China into a powerful, modern country. To achieve this result it is clearly not enough to change the productive infrastructure. Human nature too must be changed, and this is what the makers of the cultural revolution intend to do.

Red Guards' hostility to the 'Consumer Society'

The Red Guards have from the start (in August 1966) denounced those professions and trades which, in their view, symbolise the old regime's frivolity, love of luxury and links with the old ways of life. This attitude is typical of the Maoists' hatred and disapproval of everything which detracts from the essential task – the construction of socialism.
In the document reproduced below, readers will notice the resolution to abolish the fee for looking after bicycles, which marks the beginning, in the minds of the Red Guards, of free 'communist' services.
The forbidden pleasures listed below should not create any illusions about the wealth of those who indulged in them. Their cost was by no means prohibitive.
Final ultimatum of the Red Guards of the Thought of Mao Tse-tung.

1. Taxi ranks must cease to operate at once. All taxis must be handed over either to people's communes or to military units.
2. All shops selling coffins and clothes for the dead must close

immediately. The coffins must be dismantled, and the timber handed to woodworking factories.

3. Shops selling articles used in celebrating marriages and gifts must close at once.

4. Shops loaning out books for children must close at once, pending inspection by the Red Guards.

5. The system whereby cyclists have to pay a cent to have their bicycles watched must be discontinued. This service will be free.

6. Shops and individuals selling flowers, goldfish, and bird-cages, including those for pigeons, must cease their activity at once.

7. Shops selling on commission[1] are forbidden to deal in foreign articles or antiques.

8. Persons practising an improper profession, such as boxers, magic lantern operators, tellers of comic tales, or female drum-singers, must immediately refrain from these activities pending their resettlement by the State. They should preferably be sent to the rural areas.

9. All wine shops and tea-houses which are not indispensable should be closed.

10. Private doctors' surgeries should immediately be closed pending their removal elsewhere by the State.

11. Ceremonial costumes and foreign articles hired out by photographers must be done away with at once. It is forbidden to rent them out.

> Signed: The Headquarters of the Red Guards of the Thought of Mao Tse-tung, Secondary School 'Revolt' No 1 (formerly secondary school No 66), Peking.

The Chinese people seems more willing than many others to sacrifice itself on the altar of the national interest, if only to erase the image of its country's humiliation and to give it back its status as a great power. For many Chinese, collaboration in the basic work of national rehabilitation, and indeed the belief that China has a key role to play in the cause of world revolution, are powerful ideological incentives. China's future may depend on whether the abolition of material incentives in industry acts as a damper on the workers' productivity or whether socialist consciousness will be strong enough to outweigh this removal. The family plots, as we have seen, have survived the cultural revolution. This is further proof, if

---

1. These are shops where private individuals can put articles up for sale, indicating their prices. The purchaser also pays a commission to the man running the shop.

any were needed, of the prudence with which the regime applies the principles of socialism to agriculture. True, since the cultural revolution, visitors are always assured that the family plots are on the way out. It is sometimes even affirmed that they now cover only 1% of the total area of the commune – instead of 5 to 7%, which was the general figure before 1966. But the authorities admit that they still exist.

This official censure of material incentives and the profit motive was most clearly displayed during the arguments on 'economism'. Well before the cultural revolution, a number of Chinese economists did not conceal their hostility to the concept of profit as an incentive to productivity. The aims of the Plan, they argued, were national imperatives which must be achieved regardless of other considerations, provided that the financial plan, and especially the wage plan, were observed. The planning authorities did not accept that wages should be increased or premiums awarded in order to achieve problematic targets.[1] On the other hand, an enterprise was not to be judged by the profit it made. In any case, this was taken into account, and it mattered little whether the target was exceeded. The enterprise should respect the 'principle of economy' but it was not asked to maximise profit. For the planners feared that it might subordinate the achievement of the Plan targets to higher profitability, e.g. by choosing to manufacture the articles which sold best and provided the highest profit margin. In order to increase its profit, an enterprise might reduce its costs by dismissing staff, thus running counter to the policy of a regime resolved to maintain full employment, even to the extent of overmanning in factories. Worse still, the enterprise might ask to retain part of its extra profit, and share it out as a reward for the workers and cadres, as was done in certain socialist countries which regard this policy as the best means of increasing productivity. This practice was denounced by a revolutionary committee as the 'poisonous rubbish of Liberman, an intellectual in the pay of social-imperialism'.

The concept of profit, in the eyes of the creators of the cultural revolution, marks the dividing line between real socialists who intend to 'give priority to the proletarian policy' and those who 'take the path of capitalism' by giving priority to profits. This is at the heart of the fight between the two factions of the party.

1. Wages do not appear to have been increased after the cultural revolution.

The economist Swen Ye-fang was attacked because he expressed the opinion that profit was the only valid criterion for determining how well an enterprise was run. His concept was denounced as 'bourgeois', and he was reproached with desiring 'to make money', which, as Marx says, is 'the vocation of bourgeois society'. If his principles were applied, 'they would prevent the State from developing its defence industry, for that does not bring in any profit. The same consideration would apply to heavy industry and industries located far inland. A region, a province, or a town could not establish a diversified industrial system as a safeguard against the outbreak of war. In the same way, the industries designed to buttress agriculture would be prevented from expanding, for the value of their production is small, and, for the time being, at least, they are not very profitable. Nor could the State satisfy the people's needs for articles of everyday use, as these have sometimes to be subsidised. What is more, it would be impossible to produce what is needed to back the revolutionary people's struggle in the context of proletarian internationalism.' The revolutionary committee concluded its diatribe by reproaching Swen Ye-fang with 'inducing enterprises to reject the centralised guidance of the State and to proclaim their independence and their administrative autonomy'.

The cultural revolution in the countryside

Our information on the effects of the cultural revolution in the countryside is scanty. The wall newspapers published the relevant directives but it is difficult to be sure how far these were applied. Possibly only a small number of communes, especially those on the outskirts of the large cities, were affected by the movement, while others, when the directives came to their notice, did not change either their structure or their administration.

However, ever since the end of the Great Leap Forward agricultural economy was a source of discord between the moderates and the radicals in the central committee. These two factions were unable to reach agreement on the policy to be followed in the people's communes, and their continuing divergences foreshadowed the split which was to reveal itself in 1966. The Government was anxious to revive agricultural production after the famine of 1959–61, and, as early as 1961, it made concessions to the peasants which the out-and-out socialists regarded as a 'restoration of capitalism'.

From 1962 onwards agricultural work was organised in production teams, that is, broadly speaking, by the village, and the team was granted financial autonomy and powers to negotiate purchases with the trading and sales corporations. Family plots were revived in the communes, where they had been abolished during the Great Leap Forward, and free markets for the produce were opened. A peasant was allowed to keep the land he had himself made cultivable as his private property. Families were permitted to carry on private handicraft activities and to retain the income that they brought in. Compulsory cereal deliveries were assessed on a family basis. The debate on the desirability of retaining these 'freedoms' had not led to any decision before the cultural revolution. But, as the radicals gradually gained the upper hand over the moderates during 1966, it was inevitable that the cultural revolution would be extended to the countryside. This was, on the one hand, because the Red Guards were eager to do so, and it would be difficult to prevent them from moving in on the communes, and, on the other, because it was sound revolutionary logic not to leave two-thirds of the population out of a movement aiming at transforming society into an authentically socialist one.

However, even the radicals were not blind to the fact that, by carrying the cultural revolution into the countryside, they were running the risk of creating the same upheavals as those which had taken place in industry, and thus jeopardising food supplies. And if, at a pinch, the townspeople could go without oil, coal and manufactures during a revolution, they certainly could not do without food. The cultural revolution would be the first to perish when those whom it wished to indoctrinate had died.

As a result, there was a typically Chinese compromise. The directives proclaimed the need to export the cultural revolution to the countryside, but in such vague and circumspect terms that the directives were obviously meant to be applied subtly and with moderation. The ten-point directive on 15 December 1966 did not breathe a word about social structures or the organisation of the production units. Briefly, it put the poor and lower middle peasants in charge of the cultural revolution, but without suggesting any other tasks than 'exchanging their experiences'. And even so, this was only to be during the off-season.

The directive of 4 December 1967 was almost identical with the preceding one, which, it was then clear, had had hardly any effect.

In the meantime, the cultural revolution had reached its height in the towns, but there was no greater conviction in the plans to involve the countryside than there had been the year before. A few incidents in various places were reported, but only minor ones. The fear that they might proliferate, and that the factions in the towns might recruit troops from among the peasants, led the central authorities to despatch the army to 'help' the peasants – a euphemism to indicate that they intended to maintain order in the communes. The disturbances in the towns had led to a relaxation of party control, and the authorities wished to make sure that the peasants would not take advantage of this state of affairs by sharing out the stocks of food and cutting down their deliveries.

The main change in the countryside by the end of the cultural revolution – and we do not know whether it will be a lasting change – is in the personnel in charge of the *hsien*. The directive of 4 December 1967 recommended the 'assumption of power' in certain conditions, which meant increased participation of poor and lower middle peasants in the revolutionary committees and in the control of schools. The main first-hand evidence of the effects of the cultural revolution in the countryside is provided by Jan Myrdal, who went back in 1969 to the village of Liuling, in the south of Yenan, where he had lived for a week in 1962.

As in the towns, the main conflict during the cultural revolution was between the two opposite factions – those of Mao Tse-tung and Liu Shao Chi. We may assume that it was the former that carried the day, but without the struggle developing beyond intellectual debate and competitive propaganda, since the man chosen as president of the revolutionary committee in 1969 had been brigade leader and party secretary before 1965.

According to Myrdal, the major changes effected by the cultural revolution were as follows: a modification in the mentality of the members of the commune, among whom the spirit of sacrifice in the service of the community prevailed over egoism; a higher proportion of communal investments – which were regarded as a precondition of further improvements in the standard of living; the institution of a system of remuneration inspired by the one at Taching (cf. p. 94); and, lastly, the simplification of administration. Accounting has been reduced to a minimum, and is done outside working hours. There are no more entitlements to labour points. Myrdal tells us that the production of cereals, fruit and vegetables increased during the cultural revolution, and he supplies figures to illustrate this progress. This he attributes to the increased use of fertilisers, among other things, but does not give any details on that point. Nor does he indicate whether the family plots have been reduced or done away with.

Observers are unanimous in asserting that China is at present thoroughly prosperous. The cultural revolution does not seem to have left a lasting mark on the economy but, on the contrary, to have succeeded in raising the productivity of the masses by freeing them from the tutelage of the party cadres, whose zealous but often narrow-minded and unimaginative attitudes frequently had a negative, depressing effect.

A number of observers are of the opinion that since the cultural revolution China has entered a new era. National unity appears to have been reestablished. The party, the youth organisations and the trade unions have been set on their feet again. Political education has given the whole population a clearer awareness of the problems facing China and of the appropriate means to solve them.

The number of members purged from the party was less than 1% of the total, that is to say, some 200,000 people, and it seems that there were no fierce purges or deportations to the labour camps. The few members who were purged are, it appears, banned from political life and generally relegated to people's communes in remote provinces.

In the view of the Maoist leaders, the price paid in terms of reduced production was not excessive. They are convinced that the cultural revolution was necessary and that its effects have been all to the good. And foreign observers are inclined to agree.

The course of the cultural revolution in the countryside illustrates both the pragmatism of the central authorities and the firm hold of the regime. The countryside remained calm, and in most cases remained uninvolved in the events in the towns. The newspapers contained reports from certain communes where people had never heard of the cultural revolution, which shows how cut off certain regions of the country are from the centre.

It would seem that at no point was collectivisation called in question, apart from rare cases of the division of land reported by certain wall newspapers. This may have been because the army was sent to the rural areas at the beginning of 1967 and put down any attempt to exploit the situation for counter-revolutionary purposes at a moment when the party cadres might be disconcerted and discredited by events in the cities. Or it may be that the authorities' policy towards the peasants has paid off, and the vast majority of the peasants are satisfied with their lot.

8. Foreign economic relations

It would be wrong to seek to construct
socialism unaided, cut off from the world.
China will, as in the past, need the aid of
the USSR and the people's democracies for a
long time to come. It is essential to expand
at the same time economic, technical and
cultural relations with other countries.

Moreover, even in the future, once our
country has become a socialist and industrial
economy, it is difficult to imagine that we
can coop ourselves up and do without aid.

Chou En-lai, 1956

Foreign trade is the only field of the economy where foreign observers have access, whatever the vicissitudes of the regime and the secrecy in which it cloaks itself, to figures which are incontrovertibly accurate, since they are based on the official statistics of China's trading partners. In order to obtain the f.o.b. exports, we need only subtract from these countries' imports from China the estimated freight and insurance costs, and, similarly, to work out c.i.f. imports, to carry out the inverse operation (taking these countries' f.o.b. exports as our starting point). The relative abundance of data makes it possible to give a better analysis of foreign trade, which throws light on the fluctuations in production.[1]

Foreign trade has never loomed very large in the Chinese economy. As in the case of other continent-states, its share in the national product is small – about 4%. In volume, it is far less than that of countries such as Austria and Norway, and forms less than 1% of the world's foreign trade. But this trade is essential if China is to remedy its structural economic deficiencies. If imports were stopped,

1. Obviously, however, the two curves are not strictly parallel, since, quite apart from the time lag between the two processes, other factors influence production, such as changes in internal consumption or a tapering off of foreign demand for certain exports. Thus, the sustained and intense demand for foreign special steels attests the inadequacy of Chinese production, but imports of cereals do not necessarily indicate that agricultural production is falling behind consumption.

a large number of enterprises would find themselves in difficulties, and it would be hard to achieve priority objectives in the Plan, especially those connected with national defence. Even at the height of the cultural revolution, the Canton Fair, where numerous import contracts are concluded, was held at the normal dates, apart from a slight delay in the autumn of 1967.

Imports

Imports include practically no consumer goods. Apart from certain items such as Swiss watches, which are sold at seven times the import price,[1] or Albanian cigarettes, no foreign consumer goods are on sale in Chinese shops. It should be remembered that the USSR, which is much richer than China, waited for some fifty years before it bought any such goods in substantial quantities. It is therefore not surprising if the Peking Government refuses to use its foreign exchange to buy products which are not indispensable for its economic development.

Raw materials and industrial semi-finished products constitute the main import item – platinum, industrial diamonds, ruthenium, irridium, chrome, copper and nickel. Copper comes mainly from Germany, and refined nickel exclusively from France. The Chinese demand for all these products is increasing owing to the needs of the armament industries.

Imports of iron and steel products amounted to 2 million tons in 1970. They consist mostly of sheet iron in view of the country's inadequate rolling capacity, and of special steels which Chinese technology is not yet advanced enough to produce.

Cotton is imported, but this is not because agriculture has difficulty in meeting home demand. It is because long-fibre cotton is used for

1. It is curious that the cultural revolution placed no restrictions on these imports. According to Swiss statistics, sales of clockwork to China, which were 17·7 million Swiss francs in 1965 and 9·9 million in 1966, rose to 21·2 in 1967, 19·6 in 1968 and 18·7 in 1969, that is, in the years when the cultural revolution was in process. Most of these sales are of watches and only to a very small extent of spare or separate parts. This example shows how careful one must be in discussing events in China. To judge by the ethics of the cultural revolution, imports of watches should have been suspended for, at the prices at which they are sold, they are luxury articles. But it is possible that they are earmarked for the army, and are no longer offered in the shops to a privileged clientele.

the manufacture of high quality textiles for export. Chinese supplies go into the manufacture of the blue fabrics in which the Chinese dress,[1] and the ration of which is 5 to 7 metres per year.[2] China made a late start in manufacturing synthetic textiles, and has been making purchases abroad since 1967. Linen yarn is imported for the embroidered table-cloths which are one of China's export specialities.

The country's rubber requirements have been rising, and its synthetic rubber industry is insufficient to meet demand. China buys regularly on the Ceylon and Singapore markets, and will have to continue to do so for a long time to come.

In the chapter on agriculture we have discussed the extent of China's import of fertiliser.

Cereals come second in the country's imports. From 1950 to 1961, China was a net exporter. From 1961, it began to buy abroad – at the rate of from 5 to 6 million tons a year. These purchases weigh heavily on the country's balance of payments, and correspondingly reduce its ability to import capital goods. It has continued to import cereals despite bumper crops – especially in 1967 when the harvest was 200 (some say 230) million tons, which was a record. The Chinese authorities defend these imports on the grounds that the world market price of rice is twice as high as that of wheat. The fact remains that China's rice exports, which account for some 15% of world exports (China is the third largest rice exporter in the world), are only one fifth of its wheat imports. In 1971, China exported only 630,000 tons of rice. Wheat is bought from the main world exporters other than America – Australia, Canada and France. Political preferences have no influence on foreign trade. China buys from Australia, although that country has sent troops to Vietnam. The prices are kept secret. However, just before autumn 1971 Australia

1. As far back as Macartney's *Embassy to China*, in 1793, there is a reference to 'indigo, with whose blue dye the cottons used for the common people are universally coloured throughout the Empire'.
2. The quantity of the ration is not published in the press, even when it is increased. According to one foreign journalist, the cotton fabrics ration in July 1971 was 4 metres per year per person, but this figure seems very low if it is remembered that, according to Chou En-lai, the production of cotton fabrics in 1970 was 8·5 billion metres, or over 10 metres per person. Exports represent only a small proportion of output. According to Jan Myrdal, the cotton cloth ration in the village of Liuling, which was 2·47 metres in 1962 per adult and 3·47 metres per child, had risen to 5·90 metres per person per year by 1969.

was afraid that it might be ousted by Canada, whose government had recognised Peking earlier on in the year. Some writers assert that the sales of rice are part of a calculated policy on the part of the Chinese authorities. By helping to lower world prices of that commodity, China is undermining the position of the main rice exporters (Thailand, the Philippines and Indonesia), with whom China is on bad terms.

Imports of cereals fell from 6·6 million tons in 1970 to 3·2 million tons in 1971. The foreign exchange thus saved will be available for additional imports such as machinery or transport equipment. Imports of cereals will probably be phased out in the next few years.

The third main category of imports is capital goods. These were needed to carry out the industrial projects in the first two Five Year Plans. For these Plans 40% and 30% respectively of such needs were met by imports from the socialist countries. After its break with the USSR, China turned to the West for its machinery and for complete factories. The present volume of such imports is, it is true, far lower than in the fifties. In 1965, it amounted to only a third of the 1959 figure – 330 million dollars instead of 1 billion – and no order for a complete factory has been placed abroad since the cultural revolution. As we have seen, it is Chinese policy to purchase from the West not so much standard equipment as the latest technological processes and the most modern machinery. Apart from some 'turnkey' factories (that is, factories which are delivered in working order), China started in 1965 to obtain from foreign companies the licence and the know-how for certain projects, while constructing the machinery for itself. There have been cases where the Chinese asked for some of their engineers to be located in the foreign companies' designing offices and be associated with the planning of a factory. In 1965, for the first time, in a contract concluded with a foreign company for the construction of large naval engines, the Chinese technical corporation which was responsible for the negotiations proposed that it should pay royalties proportionate to the value of the production under licence.

The fluctuations in foreign trade reflect fairly closely those in domestic production, and the upturn of foreign trade, from 1969 on, is a sign of the recovery of the economy. This was also the case from 1963 to 1966, when it again reached the record level of 1958[1] – the highest ever registered in the history of China.

1. In value, but not in volume, given the erosion in the value of the currency.

It would be dangerous to attribute, as some writers have done, the present small volume of foreign trade to a desire on the part of the regime to achieve self-sufficiency. The fall due to the cultural revolution appears to have been a temporary phenomenon. In 1969, the volume was 10% above that in 1968, and was almost back to the 1966 level. In 1970, there was a further increase of 10%.

It is difficult to imagine that the Chinese Government, however anxious it may be to rely on its own strength and ensure its financial and economic independence, will ever sacrifice its foreign trade, especially since, up to 1967, almost all its purchases abroad consisted of agricultural and industrial raw materials and capital goods.

Composition in Major Groups of Products Imported
by Main Capitalist Countries from China
(in %)

	1964	1965	1966	1967	1968
1. Food and raw materials (sections 04 SITC)[1]					
Federal Germany	79·0	83·0	83·0	71·2	76·1
France	52·0	51·1	52·3	48·1	52·0
Italy	80·3	83·8	86·3	81·8	77·7
United Kingdom	65·3	71·6	70·0	65·8	38·2
Japan	63·0	79·0	83·0	83·1	81·6
2. Semi-finished products (principal) (sections 5–6 SITC)					
Federal Germany	19·5	14·5	13·9	18·8	13·1
France	42·2	42·7	41·7	36·3	37·9
Italy	16·4	13·3	11·4	14·7	17·1
United Kingdom	30·0	23·7	24·4	27·5	33·7
Japan					
3. Machines and transport equipment – manufactured articles (sections 7–8 SITC)					
Federal Germany	1·5	2·5	3·1	4·7	6·1
France	5·8	6·2	6·0	7·9	9·2
Italy	3·3	2·9	2·3	2·4	3·6
United Kingdom	4·5	4·7	5·6	5·8	6·0
Japan	2·0	3·3	3·7	4·8	6·3

Source: OECD, Series B.

1. SITC: Standard Trade International Classification.

Composition by Major Groups of Products Exported
by Main Capitalist Countries to China
(in %)

	1964	1965	1966	1967	1968
1. Food and raw materials (sections 04 SITC)[1]					
Federal Germany	—	—	—	0·8	2·7
France	65·4	4·5	7·5	—	31·9
Italy	15·7	9·0	3·0	4·7	7·1
United Kingdom	14·5	4·0	7·0	17·2	6·1
Japan	12·2	6·4	4·0	4·9	2·2
2. Semi-finished products (principal) (sections 5–6 SITC)					
Federal Germany	60·6	69·5	56·0	70·7	76·6
France	27·2	66·7	38·2	60·5	53·1
Italy	76·7	75·6	72·6	73·9	80·7
United Kingdom	42·1	48·8	37·0	49·8	79·2
Japan	72·8	64·8	78·4	79·6	87·5
3. Machines and transport equipment – manufactured articles (sections 7–8 SITC)					
Federal Germany	39·4	30·3	44·0	28·3	20·6
France	7·4	28·8	54·3	38·9	19·2
Italy	7·6	15·4	24·0	20·9	12·1
United Kingdom	43·3	46·8	56·0	32·5	10·1
Japan	14·9	28·4	17·6	15·4	10·3

Source: OECD, Series B.

What is probable, however, is that for many years to come the Chinese market will offer only a limited outlet for the main exporting countries. It was long believed in the West that China would provide a huge market for foreign products, and it was to open the country up to trade that the West forced itself on China in the nineteenth century by means which are only too well known. But the Chinese population, in spite of its vast numbers, had only a very weak purchasing power, and was perfectly capable of manufacturing, with its own raw materials, the consumption goods needed for the domestic market. The haughty reply by the Emperor of China to the British sovereign, King George III, in 1793 is eloquent in this connection:

1. SITC: Standard Trade International Classification.

'The Imperial Court does not highly prize objects brought from afar, nor can we regard all the curious or ingenious things from your Realm as having great value.'

Nowadays no other nation has any illusions about China's ability to absorb foreign produce. For a long time to come it will need only raw materials and semi-finished goods, and particularly machinery and techniques, but even these only in the small quantities which its limited foreign exchange resources permit (its imports are increasing at the rate of only 10%). It may offer quite a good market for aircraft, locomotives, lorries and electronic equipment, but not for the whole range of standard exports.

The prospects would of course change overnight if China altered its policy and decided to accept foreign credits. Certain observers are inclined to the view that the recent evolution of its foreign policy may herald a move in this direction, even though such a proposal would have been rejected out of hand at any time during the last ten years, especially during the cultural revolution. These observers believe that the Chinese leaders now realise how far their economy is lagging behind and how badly they need to strengthen their industry, if only for military purposes.

Composition of exports

Unlike the USSR, with its oil, natural gas, coal, and timber, China has no large supplies of raw materials for sale abroad. It may end up by exporting oil if its production, which rose from 1,460,000 in 1957 to from 15 to 20 million tons in 1970, continues to expand at the present rate. But at present non-agricultural raw materials form only 20% of its exports. These go to Asian countries – coal, salt, cast iron and iron ore from the island of Hainan to Japan, and coal to Pakistan and Japan. Curiously enough, the supply of certain ores, with which China is richly endowed, is not increasing though the foreign demand is strong. The Chinese foreign trading corporations sometimes deliberately clamp down on supplies in order to keep up prices, as happened, for example, in the case of mercury and wolfram. It is never clear, however, what the real reason is for a drop in supplies. This may be either a fall in production, an increase in domestic consumption, or stockpiling to take advantage of speculative price increases. Thus, no one really understands why antimony exports have stopped since the beginning of 1969. Probably the main factor

155

in such developments is the expansion of domestic needs for certain minerals. For instance, both tin and mercury are in great demand in China because of the needs of the caustic soda factories which have just been constructed.

The bulk of China's exports are agricultural, such as cereals and animal products. Rice goes to several Asian countries, especially Ceylon, but it is not always of the desired quality. The Japanese were fond of the rice from southern Manchuria which was grown from Japanese varieties, but Japan itself now has a rice surplus. Western Europe is in the market for Chinese rice, but the quantities offered at the Canton Fair have for some years been less than 100,000, compared with 913,000 tons in 1957.

China also exports tobacco, oilseeds – especially sesame, colza, cotton, and ground-nuts, which are at a premium on the world market – oils such as tung oil, and standard products such as gall-nuts. For centuries it has exported tea as well as silk, of which it is by far the world's largest producer and which it exports even to Japan.

The animal products exported by China include live pigs, pork, Mongolian mutton, poultry, rabbits, and such by-products of animal husbandry as feathers and down for the diminishing number of countries where these articles are used for bedding, skins and leather, guts, pig bristles, water-fleas for goldfish (which are exported in dried form after being collected off the surface of ponds[1]), Mongolian furs, cashmere wool, and fish, especially the large frozen shrimps and squid which are in demand in European markets. Pork is one of the products which China could immediately export in greater quantities. But although Chinese slaughterhouses are modern, there is difficulty in selling to Europe because of sanitary regulations. In general, however, the main brake on exports is, and was even before the cultural revolution, the lack of supplies of the products in greatest demand. It is therefore understandable that the Chinese authorities are stimulating 'ancillary activities' in the countryside in every possible way.

It is possible that China's main exports will at some future date consist of manufactured goods. Once the basic internal needs are satisfied, a growing proportion of manufactures will be made available for export. However, the present prospects of such a develop-

1. Supplies of this item have been sharply reduced as a result of 'the improvement in sanitary conditions in the countryside effected by cleaning up the ponds'.

ment are none too favourable. Just as the strong currency countries protected their markets against Japanese products (and still protect them against those from certain cheap labour countries), they are likely to put obstacles in the way of a flood of goods produced by China.

The socialist countries, before they parted company with China in 1960, offered much more accessible and easier markets than the industrialised western countries. But exports to that bloc under trade arrangements, especially fabrics and footwear, have sharply diminished. When compelled to look elsewhere for an outlet, China naturally concentrated on the capitalist countries. In most cases, it assigned exclusive responsibility for its products to foreign companies, some of which had long specialised in the sale of Chinese products. These companies have now placed their experience at the service of the new regime. They both buy Chinese products and sell foreign articles to China. They are not authorised to open permanent offices in Peking. (The USSR allowed such a step only some fifty years after the October Revolution.) However, they have frequent relations with the Foreign Trade Corporations at Canton, Peking and Shanghai, where they send representatives who are experts on trade with China.

The best place for trade discussions between Chinese officials and foreign businessmen is still the Canton Fair, which was first instituted in 1956. It is in the Chinese tradition to negotiate commercial deals on Chinese soil. Chinese merchants have rarely ventured out to foreign territories, whereas foreign merchants have resided for centuries in the large coastal towns such as Hangchow or Canton. The Canton Fair carried on the tradition of the medieval fairs in that town when the trade was in silk and porcelain. It is held twice a year at fixed dates – from 15 April to 15 May and from 15 October to 15 November. It is a ritual event which is essential for foreign businessmen and which indeed it is in their interest to attend. Many of the most eagerly sought Chinese export products can be obtained only at the Fair, and many others are sold at a discount which amply repays the clients' trouble and the cost of the journey. For the Chinese, who are not very keen on travelling abroad, appreciate the trouble taken by their visitors. They still welcome foreigners with the same polite formula as in the days of Macartney's embassy in 1793: 'You have come from afar; you must be tired; will you rest a little?' Although the Canton Fair is devoted both to the purchase of foreign products and to the sale of Chinese wares, only the latter are exhibited. There is a complete sample of everything that China can offer. The Fair thus enables visitors to measure the progress made by Chinese industry, at least from the point of view of quality, for many of the products exhibited are available only in small quantities, and sometimes in only one model.

The articles which China seeks to export are varied and increasing but, apart from fabrics, none of them has yet been exported in large quantities. Foreign import-export companies take a lot of trouble to obtain them, since it is in their interest to increase their turnover of goods purchased in China as this enables them to expand their own sales there by virtue of the Chinese policy of reciprocity. Chinese companies, for their part, offer competitive prices, and even quote prices below cost. However, they are still not very well versed in the art of dealing with capitalist markets, and do not always understand these markets' requirements. It is also difficult for them to ensure that their numerous and scattered producers observe the standards indispensable for any concern wishing to build up a regular clientele. Chinese manufactures have so far been sold in large quantities only in Hong Kong and Singapore, which have mainly Chinese populations. They have not yet conquered European markets, not only because they sometimes come up against import restrictions (quota systems, etc.) but also because their wares do not always satisfy European tastes. Japanese and Hong Kong industrialists have long been familiar with the needs of capitalist markets, but China is still suffering from its long isolation, and from its previous concentration on the starved markets of communist countries where, until recently, any manufacture could be offloaded regardless of quality.

In the opinion of European importers, the Chinese products with a good market in Europe are food preserves and frozen fish, and also industrial products such as small-scale agricultural machinery tractors, simple machine tools, and current models of electric and electronic equipment. The pavilions opened by the Chinese in the fairs of a number of countries aim at increasing prestige rather than trade. Chinese products are a great attraction owing to the universal fascination attaching to everything coming from China. But these displays cannot have any considerable or lasting effect on Chinese sales. For such an expansion to take place, it is essential to create efficient trade networks.

Chinese Imports from main Non-Communist Industrial Countries
(in millions of US dollars)

Countries of origin	1960	1961	1962	1963	1964	1965	1966	1967	1968	1969	1970	1971 (est.)
Federal Germany	95·4	30·5	31·2	15·0	25·0	79·0	129·5	206·5	174·1	157·9	167·0	131
France	52·7	36·4	43·3	58·0	49·0	60·0	92·4	93·0	87·6	44·4	81·5	111
Italy	39·9	29·8	19·0	19·5	18·5	56·0	62·6	73·5	61·0	56·3	57·6	56
Belgium-Luxembourg	44·6	10·2	7·9	9·5	7·0	17·0	20·3	23·0	20·0	16·3	22·8	8
Netherlands	3·7	2·3	3·6	13·0	6·0	19·0	16·2	12·0	28·8	23·0	21·6	17
Total EEC	**236·3**	**109·2**	**105·0**	**115·0**	**106·0**	**231·0**	**321·0**	**408·0**	**371·6**	**297·9**	**350·5**	**323**
United Kingdom	87·9	35·9	24·2	37·4	50·0	72·4	94·0	108·0	68·3	130·0	107·0	69
Total EFTA	**128·3**	**58·9**	**38·4**	**51·6**	**83·0**	**113·0**	**152·0**	**199·0**	**126·8**	**171·8**	**183·6**	**—**
Japan	2·7	16·7	38·5	62·0	153·0	245·0	315·0	288·0	325·4	390·0	569·0	578
Australia	23·5	161·4	97·0	202·1	153·0	198·0	83·5	190·9	88·8	120·0	128·4	27
Canada	9·1	122·8	137·0	97·2	126·0	67·5	171·0	84·4	151·0	112·8	131	195
Hong Kong	21·0	17·3	14·9	12·2	10·5	12·5	12·1	8·4	4·8	6·0	11	11

Source: OECD and Hong Kong China Trade Report

Chinese Exports to main Non-Communist Industrial Countries
(in millions of US dollars)

Country of origin	1960	1961	1962	1963	1964	1965	1966	1967	1968	1969	1970	1971
Federal Germany	69·3	39·6	39·2	40·8	51·8	72·7	92·5	76·5	85·3	88·2	84·3	89·0
France	22·7	15·9	17·0	21·0	30·8	43·6	53·8	48·0	53·3	76·0	70·5	71
Italy	24·3	12·3	14·2	15·2	23·7	38·3	56·5	57·7	48·0	64·1	62·4	63·0
Belgium-Luxembourg	9·9	3·3	4·7	8·3	13·8	14·0	15·4	13·0	11·8	12·4	10·8	16
Netherlands	21·1	14·9	13·9	15·7	19·9	25·4	30·2	27·8	27·1	27·8	26·4	33·0
Total EEC	147·3	86·0	89·0	105·0	140·0	194·0	248·4	221·0	225·6	268·5	254·4	272
United Kingdom	69·7	86·4	64·8	51·8	68·9	83·0	94·7	83·0	82·2	91·0	80·0	77
Total EFTA	102·3	118·4	88·8	79·0	105·6	132·0	151·0	138·0	138·5	160·0	152·0	—
Japan	20·7	30·9	46·0	74·5	157·8	225·0	306·0	269·0	224·1	234·0	254·0	322·0
Australia	10·5	7·1	11·0	14·8	22·8	26·8	26·3	27·9	30·0	33·6	36	39
Canada	5·6	3·2	4·3	4·8	8·7	13·4	19·0	23·0	21·6	25·2	18	22
Hong Kong	207·5	180·0	212·3	260·2	344·8	406·3	484·6	397·2	313·2	450·0	467	550

Source: OECD and Hong Kong China Trade Report

Foreign trade is a State monopoly with an organisation modelled on that of the European socialist countries. Foreigners wishing to buy or sell in China are not authorised to contact either the people using their products or those supplying the wares purchased. They must apply to one of the Foreign Trade Corporations, of which there are a dozen. This procedure is not calculated to speed up talks which in any case are usually more protracted in eastern countries than in the West. Anyone intending to deal with these corporations requires a good deal of patience and persistence. Ceremonial custom forbids any attempt to bring up the general considerations and points at once. These must be approached gently and deviously. It is advisable to adjust to this mentality. Any excessive haste is taken amiss. If the East is engaged in borrowing the West's techniques and ideologies, it has so far remained true to its ceremonious traditions in human relations.

Geographical distribution of foreign trade

It is unusual for a country to change its trading partners as radically and abruptly as China did after 1960. It suddenly withdrew its confidence from the 'fraternal countries' with which it was linked by treaties proclaiming 'the indestructible friendship of their peoples', and by technical and financial assistance agreements. The Chinese leaders were resolved to be completely independent henceforth. 'If the Soviets offered tomorrow to send us experts, we would refuse,' said a deputy minister of foreign trade in 1966. When we think how backward the country's economy was ten years previously, and how dependent China was on Soviet aid for the implementation of its first Five Year Plan, we can gauge the courage needed to take this plunge. However, since China could not do without foreign trade, it had to turn to capitalist countries for equipment and complete factories. It considered, and rightly, that western industrialists who had primarily their own interests in mind, would not mix ideology with business, and that they would be willing to sell it the most modern machinery, subject to the restrictions imposed by the Cocom (Coordination Committee of the Consultative Group, which is responsible for applying the embargo on exports from the West to Communist countries). In a few years the geographical spread of foreign trade was reversed. The capitalist countries' share rose from 37% in 1955 to 75% in 1969, and that of the socialist countries fell correspondingly from 63% to 25% in the same period.

F

In 1965 the USSR was replaced by Japan as China's leading trading partner. True, the Peking Government is none too pleased at Tokyo's close relations with America and Taiwan, and occasionally denounces these connections. But these outbursts did not prevent a sharp increase in trade between the two countries up to the time of the cultural revolution, and subsequent further expansion thereafter.

The Chinese Government is careful to distinguish between the two forms of its trade with Japan. First there is official trade, which is controlled by the Liao–TakaSaki agreement, a document renewed every year since 1962, except during the cultural revolution. Initially, this accounted for only a third of the total trade, and in 1970 it was even less – about 8%. As the Chinese official who signed this agreement disappeared in the upheaval of the cultural revolution, it has been referred to since 1969 as 'the memorandum trade'. But most of the trade between the two countries is carried on by what are called 'friendly' firms which are, as everyone realises, subsidiaries of the big Japanese companies. Thus the Chinese save face on a political level by carrying on only the barest minimum of their Japanese trade on an official level, while offering vast outlets on an unofficial level. Japanese businessmen flock to every Canton Fair. Some were living for the greater part of the year in Peking hotels before the cultural revolution. These businessmen have sometimes had to bow to the demands of their 'hosts' and pay homage to Mao Tse-tung. They may even be obliged, as was the delegation negotiating the extension of the agreement in 1970, to subscribe to declarations offensive to their government.

If we are to believe the author of *Japan without a Mask*, Ichiro Kawasaki, Japan does not fear its continental neighbour, but knows that it must come to terms with its growing power. It believes that peaceful coexistence is in the interest of both countries, and it therefore seeks to extend trading relations. It feels that in this way it will reassure Peking. However, this desire for coexistence does not divert Japan from basing its security on the power of the United States, a fact which disturbs the Chinese. It is clearly difficult for the Japanese Government to run with the hare and hunt with the hounds and, for its part, China never misses a chance of making Japan pay for its desire to be friends with everyone. It hurls abuse at its neighbour, but without going quite far enough to jeopardise its trade relations. This trade is small in absolute terms, but it is of crucial importance to China. If it broke with Japan, having already broken (more or less) with the socialist countries, it would be in a weak position to negotiate with western Europe.

For Japan, trade with China is of marginal importance. It amounts to 3% of its foreign trade, whereas the figure for trade with the United States is 35%. The Peking Government has not succeeded in dissuading its maritime neighbour from trading with Taiwan, which is a more important trading partner for Japan than People's China. Japan, with its rapidly expanding economy, can easily balance its trade with the rest of the capitalist world, from which it draws its raw materials and which it supplies with manufactures. The concept, occasionally expounded in the western press, of economic cooperation, and even of a symbiosis between the two countries, is in present circumstances a very remote possibility.

The days are past when it was possible to imagine a partnership in which China supplied the labour and raw materials and Japan the cadres. The complementarity of the two countries can hardly be denied, but Japan has found a different complementarity with the capitalist world, and in particular with the other countries of the Far East. Nevertheless, in the long run China will provide Japan with an attractive market when it has greater reserves of foreign exchange. The big Japanese companies are convinced of this, and are trying to build up their trade accordingly. In the meantime, however, it is far more in China's interest to trade with Japan than vice versa. In 1969, as before the cultural revolution, China did 15% of its trade with Japan, and in 1970 almost 20%. In 1969 the figure was 625 million dollars, and in 1970, 820. In 1971 the figure of 900 million dollars was reached, although political relations between the two countries were far from cordial. It is to Japan that China can sell most easily – and most cheaply because of its nearness – its industrial and agricultural raw materials which still form the bulk of its exports. It would be difficult for China to find other markets for its iron ore, coal, salt, cast iron or cereals (maize and buckwheat).

Japan sells the same products to China as to Western Europe, with which it competes and which it can often undercut – fertilisers, special steels, machines and capital goods. During the few years when China bought whole factories abroad, that is from 1963 to 1966, it placed only one such order with Japan. That was for a vinylon factory which went into production in a Peking suburb in 1965. If China has not purchased any other factories from Japan this has been on grounds of principle. It was determined to buy only if it were given credit, as Taiwan had been, but was unable to obtain medium-term credit from the Japanese Government. The political basis of the Chinese request for credit from Japan is clear from the fact that Peking pays Europe cash for machinery which it could have had on credit.

Japan could offer China almost the whole range of products, machines and techniques which China buys in Western Europe, but Peking considers it wise to avoid too close a tie with a country of which its recent experience has made it suspicious and whose excessive dependence on America it resents.

For China, Western Europe provides trading partners offering the best guarantees. With them there is little risk of business being influenced by political and ideological considerations. The only obstacle lies in the restrictions imposed by Cocom, which have been in force since the Korean War. This embargo on deliveries of 'strategic' products to China was for long the subject of bitter complaints by the Peking Government, which regarded these measures as an indefensible form of discrimination. In 1957, Cocom stopped penalising China in this way. There is now only one list of products subject to embargo, and it applies to all socialist countries. This list was shortened in 1958. From this time on, China has therefore been able to order from the West engineering and electrical equipment which had previously been unobtainable. It is difficult to know whether the controls remaining in force are effective. According to the Chinese they are not, for everything that is officially banned can be obtained under the counter.

Trade with Western Europe leaves China with a deficit; but this is balanced by a surplus with Hong Kong and Singapore. Hence the vital importance of these two centres for Chinese trade, and the fact that the cultural revolution had only a slight effect on trade with Hong Kong. Sales to Hong Kong began to rise once again in 1969, when they amounted to 449·8 million US dollars, representing an increase of more than 10% over 1968. After Japan, China is Hong Kong's leading supplier. However, the re-export trade from Hong Kong to China has dwindled to a trickle, since the Chinese foreign trade corporations deal directly with their European and Japanese suppliers in China, and therefore cut out the latters' agents in Hong Kong. Part of the colony's drinking water and two-thirds of its food supplies come from China, as do most of the tiles and cement used there. The American measures regarding the import of Chinese products into the United States should lead to an increase in China's

Distribution of China's Exports by Groups of Countries (f.o.b.)

(In millions of dollars)	1952	1957	1960	1961	1962	1963	1964	1965	1966	1967	1968	1969	1970
Communist countries	600	1081	1313	961	888	789	709	704	642	464	464	(401)	(420)
Industrialised capitalist countries		224	300	252	249	285	448	606	755	630	590	(678)	(730)
Hong Kong and Macao		174	219	190	225	274	360	424	505	306	325	(460)	(471)
Developing countries		194	243	217	235	303	387	453	550	487	480	(460)	(550)
Total exports	**1000**	**1673**	**2075**	**1620**	**1597**	**1651**	**1904**	**2187**	**2452**	**1887**	**1858**	**(1999)**	**(2171)**

China's Imports by Groups of Countries

(In millions of dollars)	1952	1957	1960	1961	1962	1963	1964	1965	1966	1967	1968	1969	1970
Communist countries	800	880	1268	699	479	312	386	526	449	385	385	356	350
Industrialised capitalist countries		302	431	481	426	551	687	865	1043	1180	1070	1093	1390
Hong Kong and Macao		22	21	18	15	12	11	12	12	8	8	6	10
Developing countries		178	211	170	622	191	348	410	335	347	299	398	350
Total imports	**1100**	**1382**	**1931**	**1368**	**1082**	**1166**	**1432**	**1813**	**1939**	**1920**	**1762**	**1853**	**2090**
BALANCE OF TRADE	−100	+291	+144	+252	+515	+485	+472	+374	+513	−33	+96	+146	+81
Total of foreign trade	**2100**	**3055**	**4006**	**2988**	**2679**	**2817**	**3336**	**4000**	**4391**	**3807**	**3620**	**3852**	**4261**

( )—estimates

Distribution of China's Exports by Groups of Countries (f.o.b.)

As percentages	1957	1960	1961	1962	1963	1964	1965	1966	1967	1968
Communist countries	64·6	63·3	59·3	55·6	47·8	37·3	32·2	26·2	24·5	24·9
Industrialised capitalist countries	13·4	14·5	15·6	15·6	17·3	23·5	27·7	30·8	33·3	31·7
Hong Kong and Macao	10·4	10·5	11·7	14·1	16·6	18·9	19·4	20·6	16·2	17·4
Developing countries	11·6	11·7	13·4	14·7	18·3	20·3	20·7	22·4	25·8	25·8
Total exports	**100·0**	**100·0**	**100·0**	**100·0**	**100·0**	**100·0**	**100·0**	**100·0**	**99·8**	**99·8**

Imports from China by Groups of Countries

As percentages	1957	1960	1961	1962	1963	1964	1965	1966	1967	1968
Communist countries	63·7	65·7	51·1	44·3	35·3	27·0	29·0	28·0	20·2	21·8
Industrialised capitalist countries	21·8	22·3	35·1	39·4	47·3	48·0	47·7	54·0	61·4	60·7
Hong Kong and Macao	2·6	1·1	1·3	1·4	1·0	0·9	0·7	0·6	0·4	0·5
Developing countries	12·9	10·9	12·5	14·9	16·4	24·1	22·6	17·4	18·0	16·9
Total	**101·0**	**100·0**	**100·0**	**100·0**	**100·0**	**100·0**	**100·0**	**100·0**	**100·0**	**99·9**

China's Trade with Communist Countries

(In millions of US dollars)	1959	1960	1961	1962	1963	1964	1965	1966	1967	1968[1]	1969	1970
Chinese imports from:												
USSR	954·6	817·1	367·3	233·4	187·2	135·2	191·7	175·3	50·0	60	25	20
German People's Republic	106·4	97·1	55·1	21·9	10·4	15·6	26·3	36·2	38·0	37	30	42
Czechoslovakia	99·6	109·3	34·0	11·9	9·3	9·3	19·2	22·2	13·9	21	26	31
Poland	42·9	49·9	26·7	15·0	11·2	15·0	19·2	29·6	28·5	25	18	26
Hungary	39·6	40·2	28·8	11·9	3·2	4·3	14·7	15·6	10·6	5	5	—
Romania	29·4	33·3	9·3	2·2	13·8	15·9	26·6	34·1	39·4	41	39	50
Bulgaria	6·3	7·5	7·5	3·3	1·3	1·5	1·1	1·8	2·2	2·6	3	—
Albania									30·0	(30)	(25)	(25)
Cuba									65·0	61	66	70
North Vietnam									—	(22)	—	
North Korea									—	(37)	—	
Chinese exports to:												
USSR	1100·3	848·1	551·4	516·3	413·0	314·2	225·6	143·1	56·8	35	30	25
German People's Republic	111·8	100·1	40·1	31·9	24·7	19·5	25·2	31·7	39·5	28	33	36
Czechoslovakia	95·6	93·3	41·9	25·6	29·0	20·6	13·3	23·7	18·9	25	33	25
Poland	56·0	46·4	20·7	22·8	24·8	25·0	25·0	22·7	18·7	31	23	24
Hungary	44·3	36·3	17·2	11·0	19·8	14·9	10·6	16·1	7·1	5	5	—
Romania	29·9	23·6	19·7	10·5	14·1	18·0	21·9	31·7	33·2	43	42	58
Bulgaria	10·6	9·6	4·5	3·2	2·3	1·1	1·0	1·8	2·2	2·5	3	—
Albania									60·0	70	90	90
Cuba									67·0	76	80	75
North Vietnam[2]									—	(22)	—	—
North Korea									—	(37)	—	—

1. Does not include Chinese aid.

handicraft sales to Hong Kong, since there is now no restriction on the quantities that the American tourists are allowed to bring home.

The western country which has developed its trade with China most rapidly is Federal Germany, although it has no diplomatic relations with China, it has not organised any exhibitions in China, and the Chinese Government has no political reason to favour a country which it does not spare in its press. The fact is that most of the capital and semi-finished goods which China needed most acutely could only be supplied by Federal Germany, or were available in that country on better terms than those offered by its European competitors.

After Germany come France, Great Britain and Italy. In addition to fertilisers and iron and steel products, China also buys machines and equipment from these countries.

Italy, which is hoping to expand its exports substantially after having established diplomatic relations with the Peking Government in 1971, organised a large exhibition in Peking in 1972.

The Chinese Government is anxious to have a counterweight in the West to Soviet power, and has therefore for some time expressed interest in strengthening the European Economic Community. It welcomes the increase in membership and seems willing to deal with it as an entity, unlike the USSR and the Socialist countries which have never agreed to accord formal recognition to the Community.

The contribution of the European socialist states, led by the USSR, in setting up a modern Chinese industry in the fifties was crucial. Every factory of any size in China, apart from a dozen delivered by the West since 1965, was installed or expanded by Russian technicians and equipped with Soviet machinery. This assistance was not given free, but it is only fair to say that China would never have had the technical capacity to set up new industries. The country was much poorer than the Soviets had been in 1928, and lacked any industrial tradition comparable to that left by Tsarism. China would therefore have been unable to create a relatively extensive industry unaided. Moreover, the 'engineering' (or overall studies) needed to build a factory was supplied free. The Chinese were billed for the services of the experts and the equipment, and payment was on credit. At the time when China fell out with the USSR, China's debt was 320 million dollars. Far from repudiating its debt, China made a point of settling it as rapidly as possible in spite of the natural disasters which occurred at that time. It had wiped out the debt by the end of 1964 thanks to its trade surpluses with its creditor.

Since then, trade between the two countries has been more or less balanced. But the level is far lower than before. From 1,497 million dollars in 1956, the figure has shrunk with every year until it is now ridiculously low, if one considers the possibilities open to these two large neighbouring countries. The amount was 440 million dollars in 1964; 407 in 1965; 318 in 1966; 107 in 1967; 88 in 1968, and 55 in 1969. It is worth noting that, even after the quarrel in 1960, the Soviets continued to supply machinery for the factories which the Chinese had previously started to build. These sales covered, for example, steel mills and turbines for hydro-electric generators.[1] Other items were raw materials and semi-finished products, timber and steel, as well as tractors, lorries, and equipment for road works and aircraft – five Ilyushin 18s and five Antonov 4s in 1968. This trade has now dwindled almost to nothing. In 1968 and 1969, no trade agreement was signed, with the exception of a small deal in 1968 for the sale of 20 million dollars' worth of Soviet spare parts. But the negotiations opened in 1970, the first for three years, led to the signing of an agreement – in November. According to unofficial information obtained in Moscow, the volume of trade envisaged is three times that of the 1970 agreement.

On the whole, trade with the other European socialist countries has followed the same pattern, but since 1967 there appears to have been a revival. No doubt China is now eager to show, especially after the invasion of Czechoslovakia, that it does not lump all the 'revisionist' countries together. Trade with Romania had always constituted an exception because of the excellent diplomatic relations between the two countries. In 1968, it was higher – 94 million dollars – than with the USSR, and the agreement signed in 1970 provides for an increased level of trade. However, trade with the socialist countries as a whole has sunk to about 20% of the country's total, and is still falling.

Trade with the developing world is mainly of political interest to China, and is closely tied to its aid to developing countries. China has thus been induced to buy products which it did not need, such as Guinean coffee. Its aim is to enter into diplomatic relations with the largest possible range of partners. In its propaganda it makes much

1. No Soviet expert stayed on in China after 1960, whereas a very few from other Communist countries did, but they left a few years later.

of its relations with 118 countries in order to show that it has broken through the 'imperialist blockade'. However, trade with most of these countries before the cultural revolution was on a very small scale, the main exceptions being Cuba, Pakistan, Syria, the United Arab Republic and Ceylon.

After the cultural revolution, China opened up considerably to the outside world. Thus, it developed cordial relations with the Government of Sudan. China had given that country a loan of 43 million dollars at the beginning of July 1971. After the abortive *coup d'état* in that month, and the resulting deterioration of relations between Sudan and the USSR, Khartoum turned to China to take the place of the Soviet aid. In May 1971 a gift of 2·5 million dollars and 200,000 doses of cholera vaccine was made to Chad, although that country recognises Taiwan. Trade missions from the Philippines and Malaysia have visited Peking. A barter deal has been concluded with Greece whereby Chinese sheep will be exchanged for Greek tobacco. Diplomatic relations have been established with Equatorial Guinea.

An agreement was signed with Malaysia in August 1971 for the purchase by China of 150,000 tons of rubber a year, or about 15% of the country's output, as well as some building timber. A direct sea connection is to be opened between the two countries.

In Latin America, where until recently China had relations only with Cuba, trade agreements were signed in 1971 with two countries – Chile and Peru. From the former China will buy large quantities of copper. China formerly drew its supplies of copper from the London market, but now buys it directly from the producer countries, not only in the form of ore but also in a semi-refined state. This may foreshadow the transformation of the world copper market.

The United States

Since the instalment of the new regime, the United States has been the one country with which China has had no economic relations. Until President Nixon's visit, there was no link with the United States which, before the First World War, was one of China's main trading partners, and which had always pressed for an 'open door' policy because it believed it could obtain a market for its goods in that vast country. Hundreds of missionaries were sent out, hundreds of schools opened, and, in the United States itself, every incentive was provided to attract Chinese students. Among most of the Chinese intelligentsia, America's prestige was very high.

Since the war in Korea, the United States have been constantly denounced as the main enemy of the Chinese people. They were accused, among other things, of being responsible for the blockade of China, that is, for the trading restrictions imposed by NATO on its members as regards strategic products. Since then, the situation has changed. When talks were resumed in 1969 between the Chinese and American ambassadors, the Washington Government took certain steps to liberalise trade. Non-strategic equipment can now be exported to China. Foreign firms whose products contained American material can sign contracts with her, as in the case of an Italian company which sold her 80 tip-up lorries in August 1970, to the value of 2,400,000 dollars.

This measure is perhaps the prelude to a resumption of normal commercial relations. The foreign subsidiaries of American companies in Japan and elsewhere are willing to export to China. Up till now, the Chinese foreign trade authorities have not responded to these advances. No American businessman, or member of a Japanese subsidiary of an American firm, has yet been invited to the Canton Fair, even when they have asked to be allowed to attend it. In April 1970 Chou En-lai told representatives of Japanese companies that his government would not trade with the United States, and would not grant visas to Americans as long as the question of Taiwan was not settled. This policy was confirmed at the spring 1970 Canton Fair. However, after President Nixon's visit to Peking, a number of American businessmen took part in the Canton Fair in the spring of 1972, though they appear to have confined their purchases to antiques and handicrafts.

There are other signs that the whole position has been evolving rapidly since Chou En-lai's statement in 1970. On 10 June 1971, President Nixon decided to abolish the embargo on American exports to China on a large number of products – fishing products, timber, fertilisers, coal, agricultural produce, chemical products, metals, motor vehicles, domestic appliances, and equipment for agriculture, road building and telecommunications. The export to China of a certain number of products is still banned – locomotives, oil products, naval equipment, welding machines for large diameter tubes, and jet aircraft. But it is expected that exceptions to these rules will be allowed. President Nixon has also ended the condition that at least 50% of the cereals sold to Communist countries be carried in American bottoms.

171

In this new climate, opinions in America about trade prospects in China differ sharply. Even the most optimistic, however, put the value of American exports to China in the near future at under 200 million dollars out of total exports of 40 billion dollars.

Balance of payments

Although no figure is published, we have a fairly good idea of the composition of the balance of payments. One of China's main aims is financial independence, which presupposes an increase in its foreign exchange resources. China has retained a most unpleasant recollection of having had to pledge its customs receipts in order to pay its debts to the USSR. During the first five years of its existence, the regime accumulated a foreign debt of over a billion dollars, but this was in respect of the indispensable capital goods imported from the socialist countries. In 1965 China started to repay its debt out of the proceeds of its trade surplus with the USSR. As long as it was on friendly terms with that country, China did not regard the debt as restricting its independence, but only as the assistance provided by a fraternal power which was doing its duty according to the code of proletarian internationalism. As soon as there was a break between the two countries, China decided to speed up the rate of repayment.

For now on, China is determined to avoid running into debt. Although the European capitalist countries are all prepared to grant medium-term credits for their sales of capital goods to China, as to most developing countries, Peking has made sparing use of such facilities during the years in which it has bought capital goods from the West (1963–66). Cases can even be cited of debts being settled before they were due – an almost unheard-of occurrence in international trade.

Australia and Canada have given China credits for twelve and eighteen months respectively for its purchases of wheat. The Western credits outstanding to China on 31 December 1969 were put at just over 200 million dollars. China's behaviour is in sharp contrast with that of most of the poorer developing countries, which base their plans for industrialisation largely on loans from the richer nations or from financial institutions. There is no doubt that China is anxious to appear as a nation which does not have to resort to loans, although these would have a tonic effect on its economy. By thus proving that they can develop without relying on others, the Chinese are keeping their self-respect. Indeed, they openly reproach the USSR with 'begging for credits' from the capitalist West and of being incapable, fifty years after the October Revolution, of opening up its immense resources on its own. China's refusal to seek aid, or even to accept unsolicited assistance, is almost unique in the case of a poor country in the twentieth century.

It is determined to secure a surplus every year, both in its trade balance and its balance of payments. Invisible earnings, a great part of which passes through the Chinese banks in Hong Kong, amount to some 200 million dollars a year. These are mostly funds transferred to their families in China by overseas Chinese.

The item in the balance of payments which shows the greatest deficit is that of maritime transport, since most of China's present trade is done with countries that have no common land frontier with it, unlike the USSR. Every year it is obliged to charter about 2 million tons of shipping abroad. It therefore tries by every means to cut down this expenditure by building up its own merchant navy, especially by purchases of new or secondhand ships abroad.

China has sufficient foreign exchange reserves, however modest in absolute terms, to incur debts in the event of an emergency, e.g. in order to buy cereals needed to ward off famine. Part of its resources is deposited in the banks of Great Britain, France, Switzerland and Germany. Some of it is in gold. It is not known how much these deposits amount to, but in 1965 China bought 113 million dollars' worth in London, which was flown home by the Pakistan International Airlines. These purchases were repeated early in 1966, this time for an amount estimated at between 40 and 100 million dollars. Since then, no further purchase has been reported. These transactions do not appear to be attributable to a desire to speculate, or to benefit from a revaluation of gold, but rather to have readily available a means of payment for any eventuality. China does not seem to be a large gold producer. The position before the revolution was that there were only few mines in what was then Manchuria, and their output was small. Since then, the Chinese have not released any information on the subject.

It should be added that, given its purchasing power, the yuan does not seem to be undervalued. But there is practically no black market in it. The Chinese authorities are careful to see that no transactions take place, particularly in Hong Kong, which might weaken their currency and hence their country.

China's debts, then, are almost non-existent. As against this, the country has granted loans to various African and Asian countries.

Tourism

The tourist industry has lately become an important source of foreign exchange for the USSR and the other European socialist countries, though tourism was permitted in the USSR only after years of isolation, during which fellow communists or fellow travellers alone were allowed into the fatherland of socialism.

China, after a decade in which it had no relations with any countries outside the socialist bloc, also opened its doors to tourism from the West. But this innovation, which was on a very small scale, was interrupted by the cultural revolution. It should be stressed that the small numbers of tourists at that point was due, not to mistrust on the part of the authorities (as in the case of the USSR), but to the lack of the necessary facilities, and to the endless problems raised by visits to a socialist country where tourism is run by the State and the whole approach to the problem is utterly different. In the Fifties, China had large hotels built for the thousands of experts from the socialist countries; these are to be found not only in the larger towns, but also in the inland provinces, and, without being luxurious, they are comfortable by Western standards.

The State Travel Agency (Luxingshe) organises collective or individual tours, and provides interpreters. According to an official Chinese source the number of foreigners dealt with by Luxingshe in 1965 was between 7,000 and 8,000, including the Chinese Government's official guests and businessmen. The number of genuine tourists is therefore small. Moreover, only a few towns were accessible to them before the cultural revolution. Even so, these excluded such towns with excellent hotel accommodation as Chungking, Kunming, or the towns in what was formerly Manchuria. The restrictions are due, not so much to the traditional unwillingness to allow foreigners to move about in the remote provinces, as the fear that it may not be possible to offer them all the comforts expected, and thus to invite criticism. Towns with decent hotels sometimes do not have the other essential services, such as taxis or interpreters, which are so hard to come by in the provinces. The foreign traveller has always been a rarity in China, and his hosts are keen to see that he does not go away disappointed.

The Yuan as an International Trading Currency

At the Canton Fairs in 1969 the authorities proposed to their foreign trading partners for the first time, that the yuan should be used as a currency of account. At the end of 1969 they asked the Japanese firms governed by the 'memorandum trade' to write contracts and letters of credit in yuan for Chinese exports, and in yen for Japanese exports. The pound sterling would continue to be the currency used in payments. The Japanese authorities at that point were unwilling to agree on the ground that it would be difficult to define the rates of exchange. As to the trade with the 'friendly firms', which now accounts for 90% of the trade between the two countries, this is still carried out in French francs, both as the currency of account and as the one in which payments are made.

At the Canton Fair in the spring of 1970, the Chinese again exerted pressure, and it is now difficult for foreign businessmen to refuse to settle in yuan. Since June 1969 the branches of the Bank of China quote the yuan forward, in terms of the Hong Kong dollar at Hong Kong and of the pound sterling at London, but the cost of forward operations is three or four times higher than that of operations in convertible currency.

The desire of the Chinese authorities to have the yuan accepted as an international trading currency (under the name of *ren-min-bi*) is due to the fluctuations caused by the devaluation of the pound sterling, which was announced in 1967 when the Canton Fair was in full swing.

The Peking Government took the opportunity of increasing its prestige by denouncing the instability of capitalist currencies, and stressing the stability of the yuan. The yuan is in fact a strong currency because of the absence of foreign debt (apart from some contracts for the import of capital goods on medium-term credits from Western Europe, and the contracts for the purchase of wheat), secondly the existence of gold and foreign exchange reserves amounting to some 600 million dollars or thrice the value of annual imports, and thirdly the absence of any internal debt and the government's strict financial control. It seems that the foreign companies whose contracts are in yuan need have no fear, except in the eventuality of a catastrophe, that the present rate of exchange, which is 2·44 yuan to the dollar, will be altered. The Chinese authorities are anxious not to tarnish their reputation as irreproachable trading partners.

China's aid to the developing world

China did not wait till it became the ideal of the new communism before it offered assistance to the poorer countries. It is animated by a desire to display its prowess and increase its prestige. Whereas the USSR, which is relatively rich, waited till fairly late in the day to follow this policy, China granted assistance, as early as 1953, to North Vietnam and the People's Republic of Mongolia. After ceasing to play second lead to the USSR, it has given aid on a wider scale. It is now the centre of a new formula for socialism, and it discharges its mission of 'proletarian internationalism' with messianic fervour. The countries which have benefited most from its assistance are, in addition to the socialist countries in Asia, Africa and America, regimes which, without being specifically socialist, can at least be classed as non-aligned.

As early as 1962 there were 2,500 Chinese experts – engineers, agronomists or technicians – working outside China, of whom 1,600 were in communist countries. By 1967, the figure had risen to 5,000. Chinese assistance was to some extent put on ice by the cultural revolution, but had fully revived by 1969, when forty-nine economic development projects were in hand in fifteen countries. It is not known whether some of these projects were previously included in agreements with the beneficiaries or are entirely new.

Two communist countries top the list of China's beneficiaries – North Vietnam and Albania. An economic assistance agreement for 1970 was signed with the Democratic Republic of North Vietnam on 26 September 1969. Like the previous agreements, it provides for the supply to that country of rice, steel, building materials, and pharmaceutical products. If to these is added the aid supplied by Chinese personnel, especially in railway construction and in arms consignments, this aid can be put at 200 million dollars for 1969. Aid from the USSR for the same period is believed to have amounted to 350 million dollars. What is more, it seems that, since 1970, Chinese aid has been still further increased.

Albania does 40% of its trade with China, and receives considerable assistance, so that in effect it is dependent on Peking for its economic development. Under an agreement signed in November 1968, it will be granted an interest-free loan for the implementation from 1969 to 1975 of thirty economic development projects, including in particular an industrial complex with a capacity of 800,000 tons of ferro-nickel, a 1,000,000-ton oil refinery, and a 400,000-kilowatt hydro-electric generating station. Several projects were completed in 1969, including a dam, a textile factory, a generating station and an oil refinery.

North Korea on the other hand has not received any Chinese aid for some years. Admittedly, this country has completed its reconstruction, and is now able to develop without foreign aid. It has a thriving industry, and its agriculture is sufficient to feed its population. Its standard of living is far higher than that of China, and its leaders are anxious to preserve its independence in relation to its powerful neighbour. But another communist country – Romania – receives considerable aid from China. It was granted a credit for 244 million dollars in November 1970 to buy complete factories in China.

In addition to North Vietnam, the main Asian countries in receipt of aid from China are Pakistan, Afghanistan, Nepal, Cambodia, Ceylon, Yemen and South Yemen.

Pakistan represents a special case. Peking has no ideological affinity with that country, but there is an equally strong tie in their common hatred of India. Great publicity has been given to the aid, but it did not account for much more than 1 % of total financial aid to Pakistan at the end of 1968. An interest-free Chinese loan of 107·5 million dollars was granted in December 1967 for the construction of various factories – a munitions factory at Ghazipur near Dacca and a heavy equipment factory (for sugar refineries and for roads and railways). This help was increased after the visit in April 1970 of a Chinese delegation to inaugurate the munitions factory. The additional assistance promised will cover the construction of a fertiliser factory, a sugar refinery, and a refractory tiles plant. The Chinese delegation also agreed to take part in the implementation of projects in the Five Year Plan.

In Pakistan two roads were built with Chinese aid – one from Ladakh to Tibet through Kashmir, the other from Gilgit in Kashmir through the Kilik Pass (4,830 metres) in the Karakoram mountains towards Sinkiang. It follows the route taken by the Citroën cars which drove from the Mediterranean to the China Sea in 1931. It was inaugurated in August 1969.

In Afghanistan, China has contributed an initial loan of 10 million dollars to the construction of a textile factory at Bagram, and to projects for fishery development, water conservancy and tea growing projects. It granted a second loan in 1972 to that country, this time for 44 million dollars, interest-free and repayable over 20 years.

In Nepal, the form of aid which has attracted most comment has been roadbuilding. The first road was from Kathmandu to Kodari on the Chinese frontier, running northeast. It was opened to Chinese and Nepalese in 1967 and to non-Nepalese in February 1970. Following the age-old trade route to Tibet, it is 128 kilometres long, of which 102 are metalled. It is quite out of scale with the traffic which it has to bear. A second road, 250 kilometres long is under construction. This runs from Kathmandu to Pokhara, west of the capital, and is being built under an agreement signed in September 1968 between the two governments. Lastly, the Government of Peking is said to have proposed to Nepal the opening of a third road from Pokhara to Mustang, the capital of a small principality dependent on Nepal and situated on the Tibetan frontier.

The strategic aim of these roads is taken for granted by most foreign observers. Their bridges, one of which is 200 metres long, can all be dismantled, and are built of steel capable of taking 50-ton tanks – and this in a part of the country where there is only very light frontier traffic. In addition, China has contributed to the construction of a tile factory which was inaugurated on 12 May 1969. On 9 June the foundation stone was laid of an electric factory at Sunkosmi, between Kodari and the Tibetan frontier, on the road built by the Chinese. Other electric factories are being erected in Nepal with a 75 million dollar loan from China.

In Cambodia, China has constructed six factories since starting to grant aid to that country. In 1969 it completed a hospital, modernised a paper mill which it had constructed earlier, and carried out experimental projects, in teaplanting. But the China-constructed factories in Cambodia are not all suited to the country's needs, and several of them are not running at a profit. An agreement was signed on 8 January 1970 with Ceylon for the construction of a textile factory for 25,000 spindles and 600 automatic weaving looms.

In Yemen, China has built the road from Hodeida to Sana'a, the capital, sunk wells and trained local experts in hydraulics. The Chinese medical team which began work in Sana'a in 1966 was replaced in May 1969 by another team. A Chinese mission was brought in by the Imam, but stayed on under the new republican regime. It repaired the road which it had built and which had been damaged by the defeated royalists. It is busy turning the route from Sana'a to Sa'dah into a modern highway.

With the Republic of South Yemen, an agreement for scientific and technical cooperation was signed at Aden on 31 July 1970. It provides, among other things, for the provision of Chinese technicians.

In addition, a credit for 43·2 million dollars was granted by China to the Government of South Yemen in 1972.

The work on roadbuilding in Laos and Burma, which had been suspended during the cultural revolution, has been resumed.

In Africa, where its presence had until recently been confined to a few countries, China has started work on an enterprise which is far more ambitious than any previously undertaken, and which may pave the way for a lasting Chinese influence in this part of the world.

Western countries did not regard the construction of a 1,700-kilometre railway from Dar Es Salaam in Tanzania to Zambia as being a paying proposition. However, the Government of Zambia was determined to press on with the scheme, since thereby Zambia would be able to export its copper without having to pass through the Portuguese territory of Mozambique. China seized the opportunity and offered to finance the work with an interest-free loan to both African countries of almost 400 million dollars, repayable in thirty years from 1973. In addition, another loan of 200 million dollars is allocated for local expenses (wages of Chinese experts and purchase of local equipment). The Chinese would like to see these expenses financed by receipts from the sale of Chinese wares bought on credit by the Tanzanian and Zambian state trade corporations. According to the report of a Zambian commercial mission to China, the most competitive Chinese articles are textiles and clothing. But these undercut Zambia's own industries. The two African states are afraid of being obliged to buy low quality Chinese goods at high prices. The 600 Chinese experts sent out to carry out the technical studies and topographical surveys completed their labours at the end of 1969. The construction of the line is entirely in the hands of the Chinese technicians who have 15,000 Africans working under them. It began in the second half of 1970, and is due for completion in 1975. By assuming responsibility for the construction of this Freedom (Uhuru) Railway, which the West refused to touch, the Chinese believe that they have laid the basis for their political future in Africa.

In Tanzania the Chinese have constructed a textile factory, a stadium with a capacity of 10,000, and a state farm, and have installed two broadcasting stations. The new projects started in 1968 include the setting up of a second state farm, a leather footwear factory, a hospital, and a repair workshop for agricultural equipment.

In Zambia, the Chinese have begun to construct a 380-kilometre road from Lusaka to Mankoya which should make it possible to open up the southwest region. They are busy setting up a satellite tracking station and a broadcasting station, and creating a large mechanised State farm.

The People's Republic of Congo (Brazzaville), many of whose leaders profess a form of Maoism, was granted a loan by China of 6·235 million CFA francs, which is equivalent to 25 million dollars. The loan has been used mainly to finance a naval dockyard for small ships, experimental rice and cotton plantations, a palm oil refinery, radiophonic equipment, and above all a complete cycle textile plant at Kousoundi.

An agreement was signed with Somalia for certain irrigation works. The medical team which has been in the country for several years has been strengthened, and experimental stations for rice and tobacco growing have been created.

During his visit to Peking in 1969, the Sudanese President obtained a loan equivalent to 35·8 million dollars. And in August 1971, shortly after the suppression of the abortive *coup d'état*, an agreement was signed in Peking for the financing of roads and textile factories with a 45 million dollar loan.

In Western Africa, Guinea was the first country to receive Chinese aid. Chinese experts built a People's Palace, cigarette and match factories, a groundnuts oil refinery, and a hydro-electric station, and they also laid out a tea plantation. An agreement, on which no details have been published, was signed providing for a loan to finance the purchase of goods and technical aid.

Factories have been constructed by China in Mali, as well as an irrigation network, a hotel and a cinema. New projects were envisaged in 1968, but it is possible that the change of regime in Mali has hampered their implementation. An agreement was signed with Guinea and Mali in May 1968 for the financing by China of the Kankan–Bamako railway, which is estimated to cost 20 million dollars.

Mention should also be made of Chinese aid to Mauretania (agreement signed April 1971), Sierra Leone (agreement signed July 1971), and Algeria. In the case of Algeria China granted a loan of 43·2 million dollars in 1963, and this was used mainly to build a ceramics factory at Guelma and an exhibition park in Algiers. In 1971, after the visit to China of M. Bouteflika, the foreign minister, a further loan of 40 million dollars was obtained in order to finance, particularly, hydraulic works. China is sending hydraulic engineers to Algeria and is examining the project for a dam on the Koudiat estimated to cost 204 million dollars.

In 1971 Ethiopia was added to the list of countries receiving Chinese aid. On 9 October an agreement was signed during the Emperor's visit to Peking for the loan to that country of 20 million pounds which, as is usually the case with loans granted by China, was long-term and interest-free. This credit will be used for agricultural development projects.

For some time, the only Latin American country aided by China was Cuba. Agreements for scientific and cultural cooperation were signed by the two countries on 23 July 1960. From 1961, missions of Chinese experts were despatched to Cuba under that agreement to give assistance in textiles, engineering, chemical and light industries. The mission included a leading rice expert who was to set up a model experimental farm, and one for vegetable growing. It is estimated that in 1962 there were about 300 Chinese experts in Cuba. But a crisis over rice deliveries blew up in 1966 which has affected economic and technical relations between the two countries.

The coming to power of the Left in Chile resulted in the grant to that country of a Chinese loan for 65 million dollars, tied to industrial supplies. In addition, China has purchased large quantities of Chilean copper.

Lastly, since 1971 another Mediterranean country has been added to the list of recipients of Chinese aid. This is Malta, whose prime minister, Mr Mintoff, obtained a 45 million dollar loan during his trip to Peking in April 1972. Repayment of the loan will not start till 1984.

While China's aid[1] in absolute terms is still far from equalling that of the Western states or of the USSR in value, it represents a heavy burden on the economy of a country whose national product is of the

1. According to American estimates, it totalled 890 million dollars in 13 years (1954–67), while the Soviets put it at a thousand million dollars for 10 years (1956–66). That sum was used to finance 190 industrial plants, of which only 38 were finished in 1966. Thus, the annual average of Chinese aid would appear to be 60 to 100 million dollars. This figure is 4 to 7 times less than the Soviet aid, and even less than the ratio of the two countries' *per capita* product It is barely equal to 0·1% of China's gross national product. In addition, Chinese aid is in fact less than these figures indicate since the credits granted are often not fully drawn on, for lack of projects on which to spend them.

same order as Great Britain's, especially if we remember the immense tasks still to be carried out in China itself.

The prestige obtained thereby seems worth the sacrifice. Chinese aid is in the form of interest-free or low-interest loans, repayable over a long term. The projects are mainly medium size and cover agriculture, communications, hydraulics and light industry. With the exception of the Tanzania railway there have not yet been any large-scale projects such as heavy industry plants and large dams.

China is sometimes reproached with constructing its aid factories with out-of-date techniques or inefficient equipment, and of not always producing articles suited to the needs of the recipients. But these disadvantages, whatever their real extent, are offset by the low cost[1] of the aid resulting from the favourable conditions on which it is granted, and of the low cost of its labour. Wages and travelling expenses are usually borne by the Chinese Government, and the other living expenses by the beneficiary. The Chinese personnel working on aid projects help to create an image of their country as an industrialised power closer, in many respects, to the poorer countries than are the great powers of Europe and America. They learn the local languages,[2] live simply on wages which are much the same as those of the local workers, and they do not shrink from doing the jobs usually assigned to the local population.

Will their presence not create problems for the recipient governments? There is surely a danger that Chinese propaganda and the ideological influence exercised through generous handouts of the Little Red Book will cause offence to these governments, as it did in Cuba. It appears that the Chinese authorities, realising the fears to which the behaviour of certain of their experts might give rise, have soft-pedalled this propaganda. Sudden political developments, too, may put an end to this aid from one day to another as happened in Ghana and Indonesia. In Africa, China is feared, and there are quite a few heads of states willing to raise the bogy of the yellow masses surging across this underpopulated continent. But there are also statesmen, sometimes the very same men, who imply that they

1. Chinese terms for credit are much more favourable than those of other countries, and offer the advantage of not running the developing countries into debt.
2. According to a correspondent of the Italian *Tempo* writing in 1971, the 30 Chinese doctors and nurses working in Mali learned *bambara*. Their great success with the local population is due to the confidence thus created.

are ready to play the Chinese suit if the West is not forthcoming enough with its aid. However that may be, it is certain that, with resources which are still fairly modest, China has taken its place in the forefront of the developing world.

9. China – from 'miracle' to challenge

Incapable like the sea of predicting its
surges, this nation is saved from destruction
only by its malleability . . .
　　　　　Paul Claudel, Know the East

But there is one country bent on vengeance
and justice, a country which will not lay
down its arms, which will not abandon its
fighting spirit, before the inevitable world
clash. Three centuries of European energy
are fading. The Chinese age is beginning . . .
　　　　　André Malraux, Antimemoirs

What will be the role of the most populous country of the world in
the coming years?

World opinion is badly informed about a country which is somewhat uncommunicative, and disconcerted by the cultural revolution
whose causes and aims it has difficulty in understanding. People are
therefore perplexed and even terror-struck by this country of some
750 million inhabitants which, although its standard of living is
among the lowest in the world, has since 1964 taken its place in the
nuclear club. China seems all the more alarming because the
cultural revolution has been portrayed as a series of excesses and
fanatical outbursts by the leaders and Red Guards, and few observers have tried to make a calm and accurate assessment of a
phenomenon rooted in specific historical, sociological and
economic conditions. In reality, the excesses of the cultural revolution were mostly verbal. The Red Guards may have inflicted serious
humiliations on the authorities and party cadres, but they were not
armed, bloodshed was rare, and vandalism was far less destructive
than had been feared.

In many ways, the cultural revolution was what a French historian
called the French Revolution – a moral insurrection.

As to the future, forecasts of China's rate of development cannot
be other than cautious. The country's leaders, for their part, have
occasionally been guilty of overconfidence. The twelve-year agri-

cultural plan (1956–67) set a target for cereal production of from 360 to 380 million tons for 1967, but the actual figure was at most only 220. And yet one of the leading planners, Po I-Po, predicted in 1957 that 'China would catch up with Britain in fifteen years'. This was not too ambitious a target, since the ratio of population is 1 to 15, and hence China was only expected to produce a fifteenth of Britain's *per capita* output. In fact, it is not impossible that, given its recent progress, China may meet this target. Foreign forecasts are not much help, since they tend to be either wildly over-optimistic or too pessimistic. Some observers were convinced, during the Great Leap Forward, that China was on the point of catching up with the industrial nations in a few years. Others prophesied that the regime was bound to collapse during the 1961 and 1967 crises. Perhaps it is best to set out the fundamental data on China's economy before pronouncing on its hopes of rapid development.

China – a poor country

For a country of its size and population, China's production is very small. The crop of cereals (using the word in the strict sense of the term) is only just above that of the United States, which has three or four times fewer inhabitants, and its *per capita* steel consumption is fourteen to fifteen times less than that of Great Britain.

In spite of recent advances, the *per capita* income is among the lowest in the world, and is even lower than that of many of the countries to which China is, for political reasons, granting economic and technical aid.

In 1952, when China had completed its reconstruction and was launching out on a policy of planning and industrialisation, *per capita* income was at most a third of the USSR's in 1928. In 1952, too, China's *per capita* availability of cereals was 220 kilograms, compared with 480 in the USSR in 1928 and 580 in 1913.

This poverty is aggravated by the high rates of investment, which are a corollary of the faster development demanded by the leaders. This was 22 to 26% up to 1958, 30% (it is thought) during the Great Leap Forward, and under 20% from then on.

However, although any improvement in the standard of living must be achieved mainly at the expense of investment, it figures high in the list of the regime's aims. In 1956, the eighth Party Congress stressed the 'need to increase consumption, for otherwise there would be a serious contradiction between the party and the masses which would lead to unforgivable errors'. In the difficult years following the Great Leap Forward this objective was relegated to second place. But the Chinese leaders, while determined to invest heavily, are keenly aware of the people's desire to improve its standard of living, and realise that they must satisfy the needs of the population, and especially of the peasants, if the regime is to retain their loyalty. The government therefore tries to balance its economic and military ambitions against the demand for immediate improvements. On 1 January 1970, the press put such an improvement high among their aims for the forthcoming year, and recalled Mao's dictum that 'the peasants must have more income when agricultural production rises'.

China – an overpopulated country

Overpopulation is a relative concept, and becomes meaningful only in relation to economic activity. The volume of investment being what it is, China has a surplus population, and the law of diminishing returns to applications of capital and labour is fully valid in this case. Its reservoir of manpower will not be a factor in development until it has reached a threshold of production where the country can raise its investment substantially. For the moment, the vast size of its population is simply a handicap.

After having long maintained that 'a huge population was a good thing for a country', the Chinese leaders are now convinced that birth control is essential. They are now therefore compaigning to reduce the annual rate of population increase to 1% a year. Since China's present death rate is only 1 per cent – a very low figure, little more than that of the industrialised countries, this target involves a reduction of the birth rate to 2% a year (compared with a birth rate in Western Europe of 1·6 to 1·7%). It is probable that this figure will be fairly easily achieved in the towns, but not in the countryside where some 80% of the population live. If birth control is effective, the population may not exceed 900 million in 1985. However, the size of the population is the great unknown factor in China's development, since the forecasts for the year 2000 vary between 1,000 million and 1,300 million inhabitants, depending on the birth rate postulated.

As the government can only offer a very small number of jobs in the towns to the young people reaching working age, it seeks to prevent them from leaving the countryside. It has thus been able to avoid the creation of these huge shanty towns, populated by the hordes of country people, who in most undeveloped countries crowd into the towns in the hope of finding some kind of job. The number of young people reaching working age is unlikely to diminish in the coming years, since they have been born in the years following the liberation when the birth rate was high. Will these young men and women take kindly to being forced to live in their native village or country town, especially when they have already left them to study in the towns, and then been obliged to go back in order to give the rural masses the benefit of their knowledge? Many of them undoubtedly covet a post in the secondary or tertiary sector. Their frustration at not being offered such an opening is certainly not unconnected with the emergence of the Red Guards, and the criticism by the revolutionary rebels of the powers that be. It is by no means impossible that the same group will at some future date again make its voice heard on the country's social and economic issues.

The Chinese miracle

If we are to go by such statistics as exist, and by the estimates which attempt to fill the gaps in these figures, Chinese industry comes low in the world rating. The reasons are chiefly China's underdevelopment, its poverty, and the slenderness of its resources. The 'miracle' for China has been the attainment in the space of a few years of its economic independence. It is entirely wrong to argue that, because from 1957 to 1967 China did not increase its gross *per capita* national product, it 'lost ten years'. The figures are in any case to be treated with great reserve. However, the main flaw in such an argument is that it takes no account of the technical progress made by China in that period, and of its capacity to run its economy without foreign aid.

China is now in a position to produce ultra-modern equipment and to develop the most advanced techniques, especially in the field of electronics and computer science. It is the paradox of this old country, which has entered the modern technical world only very late in the day, that although it has one of the lowest *per capita* incomes yet it possesses a first-rate élite in the field of research and development. Since it allows its people only just over the basic minimum,[1] the government is in a position to compete with the most powerful nations by concentrating its financial and intellectual resources on the most modern armaments, as its progress in nuclear and space devices eloquently demonstrates.

At present, the Chinese are making a determined effort (on a scale which few realise) to assimilate modern techniques. It is in the quiet of the laboratories and research centres that the Chinese scientists and engineers are forging China's future power. The world will one day be astonished when it learns what they are capable of.

After the departure of the socialist experts on whom China had been entirely dependent for ten years, the country was forced to acquire the essential techniques on its own. Self-reliance was raised to the dignity of a national slogan, and impressed on the Chinese people as a precondition of national independence. It is of course a costly experience. And it is certainly unusual in an age when the flow of information is increasing between countries, even between those which do not have the same ideology.

The prospects of Chinese economic expansion

It may be assumed that, for a long time to come, *per capita* income will remain low. Kahn and Wiener[2] put the figure at 300 dollars for the year 2000, but this is a pessimistic view. In consequence, the gap between China and the advanced nations such as Japan will increase. The same authors estimate Japan's *per capita* income for the year 2000 at 5,000 dollars.

If there are no unfavourable political developments, China's industrial expansion in the coming decade is likely to be of the order of 10%. But, if this target is to be met, the transport bottleneck must be eliminated and the distribution of resources between the production units must be effected smoothly.

If, for lack of sufficient investment, China cannot for the moment engage in mass production, and has to be content with a modest rate of expansion, nevertheless the basis for a modern technical economy is being formed by following, of necessity, the opposite course from that adopted by the great industrial powers, in which

1. 'We are no longer obliged to eat the bark of trees, but we are still only able to have a bowl of rice a day' (Mao to A. Malraux, *Antimemoirs*, p. 543), a striking phrase which need not be taken literally.
2. *The Year 2000*. London, 1969.

technical progress has usually gone hand in hand with large-scale industry. As the national product increases, investment will expand proportionately in volume, and it would increase even more should the Chinese leaders decide to increase the proportion earmarked for investment. A rate of 30% is more tolerable when the gross national product is 200 dollars than when it is 100 dollars. It ought at that point to be relatively easy for China to engage in large-scale production, and the country should be able to attain a high level of productivity, thanks to the training acquired by its technicians and workers. This hypothesis is confirmed by the fact that great strides have been made in present priority sectors in a short time, despite the political complications. The production of fertilisers has risen from 1 million tons in 1957 to 8 million in 1966 and to 14 in 1970, and oil production has gone up from 1,400,000 in 1957 to 20 million in 1970, most of it from the new fields discovered in the northeast in 1958.

Productivity is still low because a large part of the labour force is underemployed and does not in most cases have modern means of production. But the quality of the labour is such that its productivity can easily be raised.

It remains to be seen how long China will take, if it does not resort to foreign assistance, to reach the production threshold beyond which its development could be speeded up as a result of increased investment. Possibly about ten years. However, whatever happens, the belief that China can equal the rate of expansion achieved by Japan during the last twenty years is almost certainly bound to be disappointed. It is true that soon after the Second World War *per capita* income in Japan was very modest – 193 dollars a year in 1950. However, that figure is higher than in present-day China. Moreover, Japan entered the industrial age some fifty years before China, and enjoyed the advantages of concentrating its industries in a small territory with a consequent saving in transport investment and a higher rate of return on its social investment. Lastly, Japan renounced any intention of rearming, and welcomed foreign influences and the country's integration in the world capitalist system. It was inevitable, therefore, that it should be stimulated by competition with the other economies, by the two-way flow of technical and scientific knowledge and know-how, and by the financial facilities offered by the international system. China, on the contrary, is obliged to pay the heavy price of falling back on its own resources, and of carrying out a programme of nuclear armament. For a considerable time to come it will continue to be a predominantly rural and artisan country whose population will be poor without being wretched, and whose productivity will be low; in short, a civilisation which has not yet reached the 'consumer' stage. In China, the foreign traveller feels himself in another world and another age. The idealisation of the peasant-soldier and of manual labour, at a time when everywhere in the world the peasant is being replaced by the townsman and work is being automated, indicates the gap between the two civilisations. There are, however, islands of modernity in China where the most advanced technology is being used, and where the shape of things to come is emerging clearly. It will be difficult to bring about the transition from the present way of life and type of production to those of a modern industrial state, where the emphasis on productivity and cost is beyond the present Chinese mentality. Many a dogma now cherished by the regime will be called in question. However, the Chinese are quick at adapting themselves to any situation and, as the examples of Hong Kong and other Chinese communities abroad demonstrate, they are capable of making a great success of things irrespective of the economic and social regime.

The Chinese people and the constraints of collectivisation

It is probable that the future Chinese leaders, whoever they be, will continue to give priority to their ambition of making their country powerful, both in the economic and military sphere. This objective implies the continuation for many years to come of austerity – a more rigid austerity than in the USSR under Stalin, because of the degree of Chinese poverty. The Chinese people knows nothing of life in the outside world. As long as it has no other sources of information but official propaganda, it will presumably go on believing what it is told. For example, life in the capitalist countries is painted in the blackest colours, and the existence of those groaning under the yoke of imperialism and neo-colonialism is described as being even worse. In order to underline the good fortune of those living in China under the communist regime, the government harps on the grimness of life before 1949. The older people are made responsible for explaining the difference to the young people who have never known what the old days were like. It was Mao's main fear before the cultural revolution that the younger generation would be less convinced than their parents of the need to make sacrifices, and that they would relax their efforts. He put this point strongly and unambiguously to André Malraux in 1965.

But will the leaders, by arousing national pride with their impressive nuclear and space successes, and by developing a national obsession over the two evils of 'imperialism' and 'social imperialism', manage to get the Chinese people to accept this austere way of life and to be deprived of any art or literature except those tolerated by the Communist party? The Chinese after all have elaborated one of the most refined arts of living in history, although, it is true, the resultant pleasures were the privilege of a small minority. But the tradition is there. Will this people put up for long with a type of life in which everything has to be sacrificed to the construction of socialism and national power? It must be a cruel blow to the Chinese intelligentsia for China to become Sparta after having once been Athens. If the press is to be believed, capitalist tendencies persist in China. Even after the cultural revolution, the newspapers have never stopped denouncing the villains who sabotage the regime. There is, in fact, a latent opposition by those who are still faithful to the Soviet alliance and model, and even more by those who have never really accepted the new regime or who have rallied to it out of sheer opportunism. The Peking Government has openly admitted the fact. The account of his talk with Mao by Malraux in his *Antimemoirs* is illuminating in this respect. The Chairman of the Chinese Communist party, with a lucidity and frankness which are rare in a statesman, analysed the internal situation in China. And he emphasised the statement he made in 1957:

'A fairly long time will still be needed to decide the ideological battle between socialism and capitalism in our country.'

If we are to believe Malraux, Mao himself warns foreigners against holding over-optimistic opinions about China's future. He confesses that 'neither the agricultural nor the industrial problem are solved'. And, to one of his foreign interviewers, five years later, he declared that China was not a great power: 'It has launched a satellite, but there are already two thousand of them in space which are not Chinese.'

China today often gives foreigners the impression of a nation of robots who submit with docility to their party's and government's orders. It is certainly rare for a people to modify its behaviour as completely as the Chinese have done since 1949. Those foreigners who go back to China after an absence of twenty years are staggered by the transformation in the moral sphere. They had known a country in which corruption, gambling and prostitution were rampant, personal and public hygiene was neglected, and beggars were everywhere. They now discover a world without beggars, prostitutes or thieves – or, if there are still any left, they do not plague foreigners – a country where tips (essential elsewhere in the socialist world) are banned, where rats and flies have been exterminated, and where the towns are spotlessly clean. No other regime, however authoritarian, can boast that its directives are so unanimously observed. In China this is due to the influence exercised by the cadres of the Communist party and to the social pressure which has always been brought to bear on the individual. What we call docility is this capacity for being moulded, so characteristic of a people which has learned from its long history to cope with all situations, adapt to all regimes and put up with every kind of constraint. The most epicurean of peoples is also the one that can endure the greatest privations. But the new code has been imposed so abruptly that some doubts are permissible as to its permanence. Mao is so convinced that a relapse is possible that he decided to obviate it by campaigning against the old customs and the old ideas, and launching the cultural revolution. But, paradoxically enough, the revolution has conjured up the old devils, if we are to believe the Chinese press. Corruption, embezzlement and speculation have raised their heads again in the countryside according to an article in *Red Flag* of February 1970.

The period from the Hundred Flowers to the cultural revolution provide proof, if any were needed, that the Chinese have retained their critical approach and readiness to claim their rights and that, when they are allowed to talk freely, they have no hesitation in saying what they think. They even have recourse to humour, as in the case of the Chinese who, according to a Peking paper, reproached a member of the party with being a bad communist because, when he had a glass, he was no longer clear about the line between the various classes. The idea of freedom does not have the same meaning in China as in the West.

'As to the foreigners' criticism that the Chinese do not understand anything about freedom,' Sun Yat-sen has written, 'it may be replied that the Chinese have always enjoyed the most complete liberty, but, since they had no word to designate it, they did not have any idea of it.' There is no doubt that the Chinese people values the new regime's gifts of peace, civil order and social justice after a century of upheavals and extreme poverty, In addition, the country now has a new international dignity and prestige. From 1949 on, China has at last become master of its destinies. There is no doubt that the Chinese are willing to make sacrifices for the collective welfare and influence of their country, but there is a risk that their good will may be weakened if they are obliged to perform feats of endurance beyond their capacity.

The Maoist leaders are aware of the danger of a lessening of enthusiasm for their regime, and have accordingly appealed twice in the space of twenty years to the Chinese and their revolutionary spirit, once during the Great Leap Forward and again during the cultural revolution. Basically, they are counting on Chinese patriotism, and especially on that of the young, whose anxiety to wipe out the humiliation suffered by their country in the nineteenth century has been greatly underestimated by Westerners.

The Chinese challenge

Since their party obtained power, the ambition of the Chinese leaders has been to give their country, trodden underfoot in the preceding period, a standing in the world which corresponds to its brilliant civilisation, and to the talents and numbers of its people. On 1 January 1970, the editorials of the main Chinese papers quoted this statement of Mao's, dating from 1957:

In the year 2000 China will have become a powerful socialist industrial country, and this is essential, for China, with its area of 9,600,000 square metres and 600 million inhabitants, owes it to itself to make a greater contribution to the welfare of mankind.

Indeed, one may wonder, after reading the Little Red Book, whether Mao's main objective is the greatness of China or the triumph of world socialism. It seems that the two aims are linked in his mind, just as the battle for France and the Republic were merged in the minds of the Jacobins. This interweaving of the two ideals can be explained by Mao's conviction that China has worked out and put into practice a type of socialism which is both original and suited to its needs, that the country has become powerful as a result and that,

G   193 because it is powerful, this genuine socialism will make converts, especially in the developing world where the Maoist doctrine can exercise a profound influence. In 1915 Trotsky defined this tendency as 'national revolutionary messianism, which makes a country regard its own nation-state as destined to lead mankind to socialism'. If China cannot lay claim to industrial supremacy, it is out to achieve ideological supremacy.

This messianic concept is expressed in a rhetoric which is terrifying to many and disconcerting for all. But it would be a mistake to judge China's behaviour in the light of the often extremist and over-simplified phraseology used by their leaders and press. It is traditional in China to use a language which does not relate directly to reality. The Chinese are wild in their use of invective and dithyrambic in their praises, and have always been inclined to adopt the epic style in their politics. Besides, cannot the Europeans, too, be accused of using words wildly? Imagine the reaction of a Chinese child in a French village to a translation of the first couplet of the *Marseillaise* sung by schoolchildren.

> *Aux armes, citoyens!*
> *Formez vos bataillons!*
> *Qu'un sang impur*
> *Abreuve vos sillons.*

The Komintern, which has its headquarters in Moscow, also proclaimed its plans for world subversion during the interwar period, just as Chinese propaganda does today, and the League of Nations refused to admit it to membership.

Whatever path China follows in the coming years, it is in the world community's interest to draw it out of its isolation, even if the regime sometimes fails to make any overtures, and evades proposals for cooperation, and despite the fact that the cultural revolution complicated relations with the Peking Government. As these obstacles are gradually surmounted, China will be more and more inclined to establish the links with the rest of the world which are essential for mutual understanding. President Nixon's visit is evidence of this new trend. Its economic rate of progress will be a vital factor in China's evolution to the point at which it will be an equal partner in the world concert of nations. In proclaiming their intention of becoming a great power in thirty years' time, the Chinese leaders have modified the relations between the two superpowers.

In any case it remains to be seen whether China will really be a big power like the others or a proletarian big power which will place itself at the head of a crusade against the 'haves'. But in the meantime, so many factors may change that it is impossible to make any prophecy. As China becomes a modern nation, and power passes from the hands of the old peasant revolutionaries to the new industrial technicians, its policy may also alter, just as the rest of the developing world may no longer offer such a favourable material for revolution.

Select Bibliography

BETTELHEIM, Charles, 'Chine et U.R.S.S.: Deux modeles d'industrialisation', *Les Temps modernes*, Paris: August-September 1970.

BETTELHEIM, Charles, J. CHARRIERE, H. MARCHISIO, *La Construction du socialisme en Chine*, Maspero, Paris, 1965.

BIANCO, Lucien, *Les origines de la revolution chinoise, 1915–1949*. Gallimard, Paris, 1967.

CHU YUAN-CHENG, *Scientific and engineering manpower in Communist China, 1949–1963*, National Science Foundation, 1965.

DAWSON, Raymond, *Legacy of China*, Oxford, The Clarendon Press, 1964.

DONNITHORNE, Audrey, *China's Economic System*, London, 1964.

DUMONT, René, *La Chine surpeuplée—tiers monde affamé*, Editions du Seuil, Paris, 1965.

ECKSTEIN, Alexander, W. GALENSON, TA-CHUNG LIU (eds.), *Economic Trends in Communist China*, Edinburgh University Press, 1968.

ESCARRA, Jean, *La Chine, passé et présent*, Armand Colin, Paris, 1936.

ESMEIN, Jean, *The Cultural Revolution*, André Deutsch, London, 1973.

ETIEMBLE, Pierre, *Connaissons-nous la Chine?*, Nouvelle Revue Française, Paris, 1964.

ETIENNE, Gilbert, *La voie chinoise*, Presse Universitaire de France, Paris, 1962.

FAURE, Edgar, *The Serpent and the Tortoise. Problems of the New China*, Macmillan and Co., London, 1965.

FAURE, Lucie, *Journal d'un voyage en Chine*, Rene Juilard, Paris, 1958.

GERNET, Jacques, *Ancient China: from the beginnings to the Empire*, Faber and Faber, London, 1968.

GERNET, Jacques, *Daily Life in China on the eve of the Mongol invasion, 1250–1276*, George Allen and Unwin, London, 1962.

GUILLAIN, Robert, *Dans trente ans, la Chine*, Editions du Seuil, Paris, 1965.

GUILLERMAZ, Jacques, *Histoire du parti communiste chinois*, Payot, Paris, 1968.

GUILLERMAZ, Jacques, *La Chine populaire*, Collection 'Que sais-je?', Presse Universitaire de France, Paris.

HALPERIN, Morton H., *China and the Bomb*, Pall Mall Press, London, 1965.

HAN SUYIN, *China in the year 2001*, C. A. Watts and Co., London, 1967.

197

BIBLIOGRAPHY

HUGHES, Trevor J., and D. E. T. LUARD, *The Economic Development of Communist China, 1949–1958,* Oxford University Press, 1959.

JEN YUDI, *Precis de geographie chinoise,* Peking, 1964.

KAHN, Herman, and A. J. WIENER, *The Year 2000.* Collier-Macmillan, London, 1969.

KAROL, K. S., *China. The other Communism,* Heinemann, London, 1967.

MAO TSE-TUNG, *Quotations from Chairman Mao Tse-tung,* 1966.

MEHNERT, Klaus, *Peking and Moscow,* Weidenfeld and Nicolson, London, 1963.

MENGUY, Marc, *L'economie de la Chine populaire,* Collection 'Que sais-je?', Presse Universitaire de France, Paris, 1965.

MERAY, Tibor, *La Rupture Moscou-Pekin,* Robert Laffont, Paris, 1966.

MICHAUX, Henri, *Un Barbare en Asie,* Nouvelle Revue Française, 1945.

MYRDAL, Jan, and Kessle GUN, *The Revolution continued,* Chatto and Windus, London, 1971.

NAGEL, Publishers, *Guide to China,* 1967.

NOURSE, Mary Augusta, *The Four Hundred Million. A Short history of the Chinese,* Bobbs-Merill Co., New York, 1936.

PIGANIOL, Pierre, *Maitriser le progrès,* Laffont-Gonthier, Paris, 1968.

ROBINSON, Joan, *The Cultural Revolution in China,* Penguin Books, 1969.

VAN DER MERSCH, 'De Confucius à Mao', *Esprit,* March 1967.

YUAN LI-WU, *The Economy of Communist China.*

An economic profile of mainland China, Joint Economic Committee, Washington, 1967.

NEWSPAPERS AND PERIODICALS

New China Agency
Analyse et previsions, Sedeis.
Asahi Shimbun (Tokyo).
Die Neue Zurcher Zeitung (Zürich).
The Economist (London).
The Far Eastern Economic Review (Hong Kong).
La Chine en construction (Peking).
Le Figaro (Paris).
Le Monde (Paris).
Nihon Keiyai Shimbum (Tokyo).
Peking Information (Peking).
The China Quarterly (London).
The China Mainland Review (Hong Kong).

Index

Academy of Agricultural Science, 85, 114
Academy of Medical Science, 52, 114
Academy of Military Science, 114
Academy of Science, 113, 114, 115, 124
Afghanistan, 177
agricultural equipment, 38, 41, 49, 68, 69, 74, 77, 78, 79–80, 158, 171
agriculture, 10, 14, 62–93, 137; collectivisation of, 19, 68–77, 89–90; as 'basis of the economy' (1961–1966), 23; Five-Year Plans, 26, 27; prices policy for, 40–2; organisation of trade, 48–9; rural overpopulation, 51, 54, 56, 59, 62, 63, 64; employment, 59, 60, 61, 62; foreign trade, 62, 86–7, 88, 91, 151, 153, 156, 171; cultivated land for, 62–3, 83–84; class distinctions within peasantry, 64–5; creation of commune, 65–8; Twelve-Year development plan (1956–67), 77–78, 80, 113, 185; irrigation, 78–9; and reafforestation, 79; mechanisation, 79–80; use of chemical fertilisers, 80–3; state farms, 83–84; research, 85, 113, 114, 115; and diffusion of new techniques, 85–6; volume of output, 86–7; main products, 87–8; 1970 balance sheet, 88–93; effect of cultural revolution on, 137–8, 142–3, 144–8; see also communes
Agronomic Institute (for use of nuclear radiation), 85
aid to developing countries (by China), 170, 175–83, 185
airlines, aircraft, 99, 107, 108, 137, 155, 169
Albania, 150, 167, 176
Algeria, 180–1
American Association of Oil Geologists, 94

Anshan steel complex / institute, 100, 128
antibiotics, 113
antimony, 155
Arjenel, I.F., 105n
Argentina, 91
armaments industry, 137, 150; conventional weapons, 97–8; see also national defence; nuclear weapons
atomic energy see nuclear research
Australia, 91, 151–2, 159, 160, 172
Austria, 149
automation, 113, 190

balance of payments, 151, 172–4
Bank for Basic Construction, 43
Bank of China, 175
bank-note factory, 136
'barefoot doctors', 53
Belgium and Luxembourg, 122n, 159, 160
Bettelheim, Prof. Charles, 13
bicycles, 41, 42, 104, 141, 142; see also transport
Bouteflika, M., 180
Britain, 52, 110, 173, 185; ammonium factory bought by China from, 82; and Trident aircraft, 107, 137; Chinese scientists trained in, 110, 116; industrial exhibitions in China by, 122n, 125; and scientific cooperation, 124; Sseu-Chuan factory built by, 136; Chinese trade with, 44, 153, 154, 159, 160, 168; devaluation of sterling, 175
Bulgaria, 167
Bureau in Charge of Manufacturing Industries and Provincial Delegations, 113–14
Bureau of International Cooperation, 113
Bureau of Standardisation, 113
Burma, 179

199